Meaning and Mind:
An Intrapersonal Approach
to Human Communication

Leonard Shedletsky

Published 1989 by:

ERIC Clearinghouse on Reading and Communication Skills
Carl B. Smith, Director
Smith Research Center, Suite 150
2805 East 10th Street
Indiana University
Bloomington, Indiana 47405

and

Speech Communication Association
5105 Backlick Road, Building E
Annandale, Virginia 22003

Editor: Warren Lewis, ERIC Clearinghouse on Reading and Communication Skills

Typesetting and design at ERIC/RCS and printing by Indiana University Printing Services.

This publication was prepared with funding from the Office of Educational Research and Improvement, U.S. Department of Education, under contract no. RI88062001. Contractors undertaking such projects under government sponsorship are encouraged to express freely their judgment in professional and technical matters. Points of view or opinions, however, do not necessarily represent the official view or opinions of the Office of Educational Research and Improvement.

The author submitted this manuscript in response to a call by the Speech Communication Association (SCA) for publications on topics of increasing interest to communication teachers. The manuscript was then submitted to consultant readers for critical review and determination of professional competence. This publication has met such standards. Points of view or opinions, however, do not necessarily represent the official view or opinions of the SCA or the ERIC Clearinghouse on Reading and Communication Skills.

Library of Congress Cataloging-in-Publication Data
Shedletsky, Leonard, 1944-
Meaning and Mind:
An Intrapersonal Approach to Human Communication

Includes bibliographical references.
1. Self-talk—Problems, exercises, etc. I. ERIC Clearinghouse Clearinghouse on Reading and Communication Skills. II. Speech Communication Association. III.Title.
BF697.5.S47S43 1989 153.6'076 89-25992

ISBN 0-927516-07-1

SCA Interboard Committee

Robert K. Avery
University of Utah

John A. Daly
University of Texas

Pamela J. Cooper
Northwestern University

James L. Gaudino
Speech Communication
Association, *ex officio*

SCA Consultant Readers

Charles G. Apple
University of Michigan, Flint

Al Goldberg
University of Denver

Charles Roberts
McNeese State University

Renee Edwards
Louisiana State University

Murray M. Halfond
Temple University

ERIC/RCS Advisory Board

Joan Baker
Warrensville, OH

James Eckel
Centerville, VA

George A. Gonzalez
Pan American University

Jeanne Chall
Harvard University

Ronald Mitchell
International Reading Association

Richard P. Johns
University of Iowa

P. David Pearson
University of Illinois

Sam Weintraub
SUNY, Buffalo

M. Donald Thomas
Salt Lake City, UT

Donald Gray
Indiana University

Nancy Broz
Haddonfield, NJ

Acknowledgments

I am grateful to the University of Southern Maine for granting me sabbatical leave so that in 1984 I could go to England to study and write. As Visiting Research Fellow at the University of Sussex and the University of London, I benefited from discourse with many faculty members and students. I am especially indebted to Dick Hudson of the Department of Linguistics, University College, London, for his time and comments on early drafts of this work. John Sherblom of the University of Maine made helpful comments on an early draft. I thank Catherine Whittenburg, my wife, who has spent many hours helping me to edit this work. Pam Cooper of Northwestern University made important suggestions, as did the reviewers. I owe special thanks to Warren Lewis of ERIC/RCS, who gave my writing the closest reading it has ever received. I am grateful to my students who have taken part in the development of these chapters. Without their efforts and patience, these exercises could not have been honed for classroom use.

The chapter "Who's Afraid of Virginia Woolf?" is a revision of an article by the author, "When does fighting communicate mutual understanding?" *The Maine Scholar 1* (1) 207-218. The excerpt from the play by Edward Albee is reproduced by permission.

The diagram on page 98 and adapted for the cover design is taken from B. A. Fisher, *Interpersonal Communications: Pragmatics of Human Relationships* (New York: Random House, 1987).

About the Author

Leonard J. Shedletsky is Associate Professor at the University of Southern Maine (Portland), where he chairs the Department of Communication. He was born on April 4, 1944, and raised in New York City. His undergraduate study in Speech and Theatre was done at Brooklyn College. He has done graduate work in Telecommunications at the University of Southern California, and received the M.A. degree in Broadcast Communication Arts from San Francisco State College. He wrote his Ph.D. dissertation at the University of Illinois; it concerns the effects of some clause variables on memory-scanning. He has lectured widely and published extensively on a variety of subjects relating to intrapersonal communication; he has taught and done research at universities in the United States and England.

*In memory of
Jennifer Sheldon*

Table of Contents

Part I   Page

Introduction 1
The Journal 3
"Who's Afraid of Virginia Woolf?" 6
Silence (1): Focus on Thinking 13
Silence (2): Thinking about Focus 16
Group Discussion 19
Mental Dynamics 22
    Linguistic Intuition:
    Conscious versus Nonconscious
    Mental Processing 23
Biofeedback 29
    Temperature Control 29
    Relaxation of Muscular Tension 30
Depth of Processing 31
Reconstruction from Memory: Inference 44
Active versus Passive Processing 57
Concept Formation 61
    (1) Concept Identification:
        Physical Attributes 61
    (2) Concept Identification:
        Semantic Attributes 65
        Meaning (a) 65
        Meaning (b) 67
        Syntax/Meaning 68

Table of Contents (Continued)

Self-Concept 69
Analysis of Verbal Codes 71
    Phonological Coding
    in Immediate Memory 71
    Visual versus Verbal Coding 73
Individual Differences 76
    Cognitive Style 77
    Direction of Gaze 79
Ideal Self-Description 84
Social Cognition 88
    Accounts 88

Part II

A Reflection on the Mind at Work 90
A Sampler of Definitions 91
Intrapersonal Communication
Is More Than Just Talking
to Yourself 94
Intrapersonal Communication
Is at the Center of All Communication 97
A Receiver-Based Definition
of Intrapersonal Communication 101
Assigning Meaning 102
Mind as Information Processor 105
References 108
Author Index 115
Subject Index 117

Part I

Introduction

The key to an effective course or unit on intrapersonal communication is student participation. The student will learn best when he or she actively processes the ideas presented. The metacognition itself involved in becoming aware of one's own mental processing facilitates learning. This is one of the most important lessons we learn from cognition. The student must apply the concepts learned, ask questions about them, intellectually wrestle with them, speculate about them, and observe their manifestation in his/her own experience. (See Popper, 1972.) It is one thing to read about selective attention and quite another to "catch" oneself shifting attention in the course of a conversation; to know that words can be ambiguous, and to experience ambiguity and alternative interpretations in communication; to learn about emotions, and to observe one's own emotional triggers and their effects upon reasoning. (See William James, 1890.)

The exercises presented here are certainly not intended to exhaust the possibilities or to define intrapersonal communication utterly. They have been chosen because they help to demonstrate interesting, theoretically relevant, and doable classroom activities. At one time or another, I have used every one of these exercises in the classroom; and at times, some of these tasks have been part of my research. I do not use all of these exercises every time I teach intrapersonal communication. Depending on which text is being used and the particular interest that develops in the class, different exercises are employed. Some of these exercises, however, have become a staple in my course on intrapersonal communication. For instance, "The Journal" exercise is built into the syllabus and is always an important component of the course. I have used many of these exercises in related courses; for example, "Silence" is effective in a component on intrapersonal communication in an

Introduction to Communication course, and "Group Discussion" and "Reconstruction from Memory" are relevant and effective in courses devoted to linguistic behavior. The intra- personal aspects of these exercises are salient across a wide range of courses.

The exercises are presented here with introductory comments, a statement of goals, instructions, materials, and analysis. The purpose of the analysis section of each exercise is to help you with discussion of the exercise. A brief description of what the exercise demonstrates, questions that facilitate discussion, related concepts, some discussion of theory, and relevant citations are provided. In the exercises where handouts for your students are required, I have designed the page so that you can easily and efficiently photocopy the needed material. The exercises invariably spark interest and ignite speculation and discussion. Students enjoy and benefit from these experiences. Having experienced a phenomenon, they are interested in understanding how it works.

The Journal

Introduction

The central exercise in learning about one's own intrapersonal communication is keeping "The Journal." This journal is an open-ended record of any and all intrapersonal experiences that the students wish to record. Some will pursue an underlying theme throughout most of their entries; others will skip about, influenced by course materials and their own shifting foci. Regardless of style, the students will find the journal extremely useful in bringing the course concepts alive, in finding an interesting topic for a term paper, and in gaining a view of the often overlooked universe within, the boundless possibilities of one's own mind.

Goals: The journal serves three main purposes:

(1) to motivate the student to observe him/herself

(2) to increase awareness of, and control over, intrapersonal communication

(3) to allow the student an unstructured arena in which to explore a wide range of intrapersonal behaviors, some of which are mostly private (e.g., emotions, attitudes, physiological reactions, confusions, and more).

Approach: Students are asked to keep an intrapersonal communication journal. A separate notebook exclusively for this purpose is best. To protect their privacy, they may wish to use notebooks that allow them to remove pages when the journal is handed in. The basic instruction for keeping the journal is simple: "Notice when you've experienced an intrapersonal event, and write about it—describe it, discuss how it fits with the larger context of your mind, and how it influences your behavior."

As with most journals and relatively unstructured exercises, the beginning may be slow and awkward, but a major payoff comes with giving the students room to find their own intrapersonal communication. You can aid the process in a number of ways:

(1) Devote class time early in the semester to students who wish to speak about their journal entries.

(2) Offer your own recent intrapersonal experiences as examples of potential journal entries.

(3) Generate ideas in class for journal topics from readings, discussion, and handouts—such as listening, dreams, daydreams, emotional triggers, musical experiences, pain, smells, touch, physiological reactions, stress, associations, forgetting, selective attention, distractions, ambiguous interpretations, tip-of-the-tongue and slip-of-the-tongue experiences, feelings about oneself, errors, sometime "automatic" behaviors (like driving, thought during deep involvement in an activity, and others), and self-dialogue. (See Edwards, Honeycutt, & Zagacki, 1988, for an excellent empirical study of self-dialogue.)

(4) Supply students with samples of student journal entries.

(5) Provide students with suggested, structured exercises (for instance, see Barker & Edwards, 1980; Dauw, 1980; or any of the exercises in this book). You might encourage students to select a listening context (i.e., a person or a situation—e.g., lectures) and to track their intrapersonal behavior while they listen, to catch themselves, and to write about their behavior. The key here is to get the students writing and to give them immediate feedback so they can know that they are on track. Let them know that it is all right to explore. Consider these entries from student journals:

*****

Listening, do I listen? Most times I do. Since Tuesday I have become so aware of my listening habits. I do get distracted in class by things I don't understand and my mind goes to things I do understand. The past three days I have become aware of how outside stimuli effect [sic] me when I'm in my car. How I react to the things they do that I think are stupid. I become angry, only for a few seconds, but angry none the less.

To some degree I have a low tolerance for ambiguity. I usually want clear-cut easily defined situations. I want to know where I stand and then I'll decide what I'll do about it.

On the locus of control my feelings are varied. I believe God has a plan for each of us but that I with Him am the master of my fate, that certain changes can be made and I must accept the consequences of my decisions and if what happens is contrary to what I thought I wanted, to adjust myself to that until another choice comes along. I would consider myself an internal because I do not believe outside forces can control my life. Rain, snow, etc., but doesn't control what goes on inside me, my intrapersonal relationships.

* * * * *

What a relief to find out I was not the only one who did not grasp what Condon is talking about. But even better than that to be told that concrete people have a problem with semantics. I've been doing such a mental put down on myself, thinking I was stupid, dumb, to the point of thinking maybe I should just leave school and get a job because I don't have what it takes to grasp this intellectual ideal. I didn't even admit to myself what I was doing to myself, or maybe I wasn't aware of what I was doing. It was as if a weight were lifted off me and once the fear of stupidity was removed, I could be objective. Not understanding one book does not make me stupid.

"Who's Afraid of Virginia Woolf?"

Goals: This exercise demonstrates through analysis of dialogue that talk consists of levels, or types, of meaning. For instance, both literal meaning and interpersonal meaning occur in talk. However, the distance between what is said and what is meant (or understood to have been said and meant) may be great. The exercise helps to show that the interpersonal domain of talk interfaces with the intrapersonal domain of assigning meaning.

Approach: If you can show the videotape of "Who's Afraid of Virginia Woolf?" or even play the audio version, you will certainly enrich the experience.

Step 1. Ask the class to read the opening lines of "Who's Afraid of Virginia Woolf?" (Albee, 1962, reproduced below). Next, ask the students to write a brief interpretation of what the conversation is about, i.e., what Martha is trying to do and what George is trying to do in this dialogue. What does each seem to understand from the conversation? This writing is in preparation for a class discussion that pits the literal interpretation against the interpersonal interpretation of the dialogue.

Interpretation 1: Literal Meaning

George and Martha, the main characters in Albee's drama, are discussing the name of a Bette Davis film. Martha insists that George remember the name of the film. George is tired and wants to go to bed.

Interpretation 2: Interpersonal Meaning

Martha is trying to tell George, indirectly, that she is discontent with their marriage, that he is inadequate in performing his role. She does this by drawing a parallel between their marriage and the characters in the Bette Davis film that she is describing to George. George fully understands Martha, but purposely refuses to acknowledge her message, because he enjoys frustrating her. Martha may well know what George is doing, but she does not know how to engage him in the issues about which she is trying to communicate.

Step 2. Divide the class by a show of hands into those who believe that Interpretation 1 is correct, and those who believe that Interpretation 2 is correct. Generate discussion in the attempt to resolve the literal versus the interpersonal meaning in the dialogue.

Step 3. If it is not feasible to show the videotape or play the audiotape, you may wish to read from the play or have the students read the opening lines from the play. Here is the opening scene of the play:

MARTHA	(1) *JESUS...*
GEORGE	(2) ...SHHHHHHH
MARTHA	(3) ...H. CHRIST...
GEORGE	(4) FOR GOD'S SAKE, MARTHA, IT'S TWO O'CLOCK IN THE...
MARTHA	(5) OH, GEORGE!
GEORGE	(6) WELL, I'M *SORRY*, BUT...
MARTHA	(7) WHAT A CLUCK! WHAT A CLUCK YOU ARE.
GEORGE	(8) IT'S LATE, YOU KNOW? LATE.
MARTHA	(9) **(LOOKS ABOUT THE ROOM. IMITATES BETTE DAVIS)** WHAT A DUMP. HEY, WHAT'S THAT FROM? "WHAT A DUMP?"
GEORGE	(10) HOW WOULD I KNOW...
MARTHA	(11) AW, COME ON! WHAT'S IT FROM? *YOU* KNOW...

GEORGE	(12) ...MARTHA...
MARTHA	(13) *WHAT'S IT FROM, FOR CHRIST'S SAKE?*
GEORGE	(14) **(WEARILY)** WHAT'S WHAT FROM?
MARTHA	(15) I JUST TOLD YOU; I JUST DID IT. "WHAT A DUMP!" HUNH? WHAT'S THAT FROM?
GEORGE	(16) I HAVEN'T THE FAINTEST IDEA WHAT...
MARTHA	(17) DUMBBELL! IT'S FROM SOME GODDAMN BETTE DAVIS PICTURE... SOME GODDAMN WARNER BROTHERS EPIC...
GEORGE	(18) *I CAN'T* REMEMBER ALL THE PICTURES THAT...
MARTHA	(19) NOBODY'S ASKING YOU TO REMEMBER EVERY SINGLE GODDAMN WARNER BROTHERS EPIC...JUST ONE! ONE SINGLE LITTLE EPIC! BETTE DAVIS GETS PERITONITIS IN THE END...SHE'S GOT THIS BIG BLACK FRIGHT WIG SHE WEARS ALL THROUGH THE PICTURE AND SHE GETS PERITONITIS, AND SHE'S MARRIED TO JOSEPH COTTEN OR SOMETHING...
GEORGE	(20) ...SOME*BODY*...
MARTHA	(21) ...SOMEBODY...AND SHE WANTS TO GO TO CHICAGO ALL THE TIME, 'CAUSE SHE'S IN LOVE WITH THAT ACTOR WITH THE SCAR...BUT SHE GETS SICK AND SHE SITS DOWN IN FRONT OF HER DRESSING TABLE...
GEORGE	(22) WHAT ACTOR? WHAT SCAR?
MARTHA	(23) I CAN'T REMEMBER HIS NAME, FOR GOD'S SAKE. WHAT'S THE NAME OF THE *PICTURE*? I WANT TO KNOW WHAT THE NAME OF THE *PICTURE* IS. SHE SITS DOWN IN FRONT OF HER DRESSING TABLE...AND SHE'S GOT THIS PERITONITIS...AND SHE TRIES TO PUT HER LIPSTICK ON, BUT SHE DECIDES TO GO TO CHICAGO ANYWAY, AND...

GEORGE	(24) *CHICAGO!* IT'S CALLED *CHICAGO*.
MARTHA	(25) HUNH? WHAT...WHAT IS?
GEORGE	(26) THE PICTURE...IT'S CALLED CHICAGO...
MARTHA	(27) GOOD GRIEF! DON'T YOU KNOW *ANYTHING*? *CHICAGO* WAS A 'THIRTIES MUSICAL, STARRING LITTLE MISS ALICE *FAYE*. DON'T YOU KNOW *ANYTHING*?
GEORGE	(28) WELL, THAT WAS PROBABLY BEFORE MY *TIME*, BUT...
MARTHA	(29) CAN IT! JUST CUT THAT OUT! THIS PICTURE...BETTE DAVIS COMES HOME FROM A HARD DAY AT THE GROCERY STORE...
GEORGE	(30) SHE WORKS IN A GROCERY STORE?
MARTHA	(31) SHE'S A HOUSEWIFE; SHE BUYS THINGS...AND SHE COMES HOME WITH THE GROCERIES, AND SHE WALKS INTO THE MODEST LIVING ROOM OF THE MODEST COTTAGE MODEST JOSEPH COTTEN SET HER UP IN...
GEORGE	(32) ARE THEY MARRIED?
MARTHA	(33) **(IMPATIENTLY)** YES. THEY'RE MARRIED. TO EACH OTHER. CLUCK! AND SHE COMES IN, AND SHE LOOKS AROUND, AND SHE PUTS HER GROCERIES DOWN, AND SHE SAYS, "WHAT A DUMP."
GEORGE	(34) **(PAUSE)** OH.
MARTHA	(35) **(PAUSE)** SHE'S DISCONTENT.
GEORGE	(36) **(PAUSE)** OH.
MARTHA	(37) **(PAUSE)** WELL, WHAT'S THE NAME OF THE PICTURE?
GEORGE	(38) I REALLY DON'T KNOW, MARTHA...
MARTHA	(39) WELL, THINK!

GEORGE   (40) I'M TIRED, DEAR...IT'S LATE...AND BESIDES...

MARTHA   (41) I DON'T KNOW WHAT YOU'RE SO TIRED ABOUT...YOU HAVEN'T *DONE* ANYTHING ALL DAY; YOU DIDN'T HAVE ANY CLASSES, OR ANYTHING...

Analysis

It is likely that the reader is asking, Is this an exercise in intrapersonal or interpersonal communication? In what way(s) is this an exercise in intrapersonal communication? We often start with an intrapersonal focus and soon find ourselves squarely in the midst of interpersonal issues—all the more so, perhaps, because of the often private and personal domain of the intrapersonal. Simultaneous with the interpersonal dimensions evident in the play, we have a good example of how conversations and relationships are constructed by information processors.

The interpersonal meaning of Interpretation 2 attributes a considerable amount of cognitive activity to George and Martha (as well as to the audience). In order to understand how George and Martha, and the rest of us, construct meaning and build interpersonal relationships, we need to understand how meaning is encoded and decoded. The more indirect the meaning, the more clear it is that simple, mechanistic accounts of communication are inadequate.

Accounts of interpersonal/intrapersonal meaning can be found in the literature of discourse analysis, conversational analysis, and pragmatics. For an insightful description of the interpretive machinery that may lie behind the conversation, see Tannen (1988). Tannen makes clear how talk may be categorized by style and thus produce its own set of messages, leading to rapport or conflict. While the analyst can make explicit much of the machinery behind conversational behavior, the ordinary language user can, of course, run all of the mental machinery intuitively. (See also Labov & Fanshel, 1977; Joshi, Webber, & Sag, 1981; Brown & Yule, 1983; Craig & Tracy, 1983; Levinson, 1983; McLaughlin, 1984; and many others.)

Intriguing in the episode between George and Martha is that the reader intuitively senses that George and Martha understand one another extremely well. George understands the parallel that Martha is drawing, and Martha understands George's refusal to acknowledge his understanding. Moreover, they know that they understand one another, that is, they have mutual knowledge. None of this is stated literally, and yet they understand one another; and we know they do, although at this early point in the play, we are not certain quite what they have communicated to one another. The question that I would like to raise is this: How can we explain a form of communication in which the literal meaning (e.g., the question, "She works in a grocery store?") and the meaning communicated (e.g., "I do not understand the point you are making", or "I refuse to acknowledge your point") are distant from one another? The real challenge before us is to discover what is available within our own minds to analyze interactions like these. Where do our intuitions come from? We all sense more than literal meaning in what is said, but how do we do that?

Consider George's reaction to Martha's anger over his "before my time" utterance (line 28). Following Martha's insistence that they return to the topic of the picture, George asks: "She works in a grocery store?" In this manner, George complies with Martha by asking a question about the plot. However, his question adds to Martha's anger. And when we look at it more closely, we begin to see why. His question suggests that George does not really follow what Martha is talking about, and this is highly frustrating to her.

But what is she talking about? Is she really talking about a Bette Davis picture? No, she is talking about George's and her marriage. She is talking about herself and him by drawing parallels between themselves and the movie characters. Any misunderstanding on George's part communicates that he has missed this parallel or that he is unwilling to acknowledge it. Hence, Martha is angry when George asks if the character works in a grocery store, as opposed to being a housewife who shops in one, as Martha does.

    We see that the hearer (George) is reacting to the underlying, or global, topic (a married couple much like George and Martha) and to the underlying goal of the speaker (Martha), which is to communicate her discontentment, rather than to chat about the surface topics. Discontent is the connection between the global topic and the speaker's underlying goal. In this case, the hearer is purposely frustrating the speaker in her attempt to achieve her goal. Moreover, I suggest that the speaker knows that the hearer is purposely frustrating her. Why do I say that she knows that he is aware of her intentions and is *purposely* trying to obstruct them? The answer to this question is much like the answer to how Martha knows how to interpret George's "before my time" utterance—it is the conclusion I come to after following a reasoned process of trying to uncover possible implications in the dialogue.

    You may wish to discuss how one might support, or negate, the claim that George is purposely trying to frustrate Martha's goals. Have fun!

Silence (1): Focus on Thinking

Goal: To generate thinking about thought. This exercise provides a common experiential base from which your class can discuss the functions and effects of ordinary thought, especially verbal thought.

Approach: Ask the class to not-think for fifteen minutes. What this means is for them to stop thinking with words or meaningful images. Mental awareness about random noise is permitted. Point out in advance that untrained people rarely, if ever, are able to not-think for fifteen minutes. Fifteen minutes sounds like a lot of time for this task, but, interestingly, when it is over, many of the participants will report that they found the time seemed to go faster than usual. Also, participants need the time to go through the stages of struggling with the task, finding strategies that work, and relaxing. It is okay if anyone chooses not to take part in this exercise. Rarely do people take this option, but for some it is important to feel that they are not obliged to do this exercise.

If your room is a particularly quiet and friendly place, that is good; but I have performed the silence exercise in ordinary classrooms for years. Leave the room during the fifteen minutes, promising to come back at the end of the time, when you will gently ask people to return to ordinary consciousness. The reason for leaving the room is because participants are likely to be more comfortable without someone watching them. The promise to "awaken" the group gently is simply to facilitate their letting-go by assuring them that they will not be jarred abruptly from a restful state.

When you return to the room, quietly ask people to "wake up," and allow them a few minutes to reorient themselves. Then ask for volunteers to share information on the experience. They typically will say that they could not achieve not-thinking for any stretch of time; that they were fighting within themselves, between the self-instruction, "Don't think!" and the thought, "Oops, I'm thinking."

Analysis

Discussion can be facilitated by raising the following topics: relaxation, psychological time, involuntary naming, and heightened sensation. Generally, a large segment of the group will have experienced relaxation. (See Bensen, 1975.) Approximately half or more will have experienced the fifteen minutes as going fast, in spite of having thought beforehand that fifteen minutes sounded like a long time to not-think. Most or all will have experienced involuntary naming, i.e., the experience of naming events or objects in spite of the attempt to not-think with words. Naming is part of our mental being. Finally, many will report a heightened awareness of sounds, tactile sensations, and other stimuli that were present all along but that were not noticed earlier. This may lead to a discussion of selective attention, i.e., the moment-by-moment editing that we do to the stimuli that constantly flow into us.

After I conduct the silence exercise, I read two paragraphs from Susanne Langer's *Philosophy in a New Key*, which contain Helen Keller's reminiscences about the dawn of "Language" in her experience of acquiring the concept "word." This leads to a discussion of signs and symbols and to a discussion of concept formation (see the exercise on concept formation, p. 61). Langer (1942) wrote:

> There is a famous passage in the autobiography of Helen Keller, in which this remarkable woman describes the dawn of Language upon her mind. Of course she had used signs before, formed associations, learned to expect things and identify people or places; but there was a great day when all sign-meaning was eclipsed and dwarfed by the discovery that a certain datum in her limited sense-world had a *denotation*, that a particular act of her fingers constituted a *word*. This event had required a long preparation; the child had learned many

finger acts, but they were as yet a meaningless play. Then, one day, her teacher took her out to walk—and there the great advent of Language occurred.

"She brought me my hat," the memoir reads, "and I knew I was going out into the warm sunshine. This thought, if a wordless sensation may be called a thought, made me hop and skip with pleasure.

"We walked down the path to the well-house, attracted by the fragrance of the honeysuckle with which it was covered. Some one was drawing water and my teacher placed my hand under the spout. As the cool stream gushed over my hand she spelled into the other the word *water*, first slowly, then rapidly. I stood still, my whole attention fixed upon the motion of her fingers. Suddenly I felt a misty consciousness as of something forgotten—a thrill of returning thought; and somehow the mystery of language was revealed to me. I knew then that w-a-t-e-r meant the wonderful cool something that was flowing over my hand. That living word awakened my soul, gave it light, hope, joy, set it free! There were barriers still, it is true, but barriers that in time could be swept away.

"I left the well-house eager to learn. Everything had a name, and each name gave birth to a new thought. As we returned to the house every object which I touched seemed to quiver with life. That was because I saw everything with the strange, new sight that had come to me."

Silence (2): Thinking about Focus

In this exercise, proposed by Lyall Crawford (1989), people remain silent as they explore their own thoughts during a social encounter. This exercise has been used to open a basic course in interpersonal communication, to encourage an atmosphere of exploration.

Goals: To encourage students to monitor themselves as they begin to explore self-perception and their perceptions of others.

Approach: The following handout is given to the students and with it the exercise begins.

Analysis

Clearly, this exercise on silence, in contrast to the preceding one, emphasizes the role of intrapersonal processes in social encounters. It raises to consciousness our reactions to a social encounter, which may include physiological, emotional, and ideational components. We consider our information processing—what we pay attention to, and how we think about what we notice. It raises for discussion our style of developing ideas about ourselves and others.

Please do not talk.

Read this instead.

The quarter has begun. This is our first class together. Instead of talking from the very beginning, which is what we commonly do when we first meet someone, let us begin our contact with one another by being silent.

For the next twenty minutes or so, quiet yourself. Become mindful of what you are feeling and thinking. Try to make yourself aware of everything that is happening in your experience. Become the object of your own cognition. Close your eyes, if this will help you focus your attention intrapersonally. When you attend to yourself in this way, what cognitive and non-cognitive occurrences take place? Do you feel uncomfortable or silly sitting in a room with other people and behaving in this manner? Are you uneasy with being quiet and contemplative? Pay attention to your paying attention. Remember what you notice.

Next, move your focus from the inside to the outside. Position yourself so you can look around the room and see everyone present. Put your attention on the other persons who have enrolled in this class with you. What do you notice? Take paper and pencil and write down your impressions. Record at least one impression for everyone in the class with you. Are they mostly strangers or have you signed up for this class with many of your friends? Is there someone present you find particularly attractive? Is there someone present you cannot imagine yourself having anything in common with? What do you actually notice about others, especially during initial encounters? Do you seem to focus on the same characteristics, no matter what the situation or the person encountered? What information do you use to form your impressions of other persons? When you consider your present situation, are you generally pleased or generally disappointed with what you discover when you look around the room? How does this affect your expectations for this class? What are your reasons for being here, anyway? Or maybe you are not thinking along these lines at all. If this is the case, what are you thinking? Feeling? Record what is going on. Remember, you should have at least one impression of everyone present with you in the classroom.

Begin as soon as you have read these instructions. All too soon our quiet time together will end.

Group Discussion

Goals: This exercise shows that group members give widely different interpretations of one another's utterances, and that they often are not aware of this disparity.

Approach: Ask the class to take part in a small group discussion that will be tape-recorded. Ask students to discuss course material; "listening" is a good topic—it fits well with this exercise. Tape-record the discussion and transcribe part of it, perhaps ten speaking turns. You may wish to have the students do the transcription in class. Either in class or as a homework assignment, have each student write out what they individually think each utterance meant, or how it functioned in the conversation, and what it connected with in the conversation. Compare notes and determine whether people agree or disagree about what was going on in the conversation. Typically, a good deal of variation in interpretation shows up. The following is an exact transcription of two students (A and B) and the teacher discussing listening and turn-taking, while the rest of the class listened and watched.

10/14/87

(1) Student A: ...when my right goes against your right, you're going to think I'm wrong automatically—ah, you might listen to me...

(2) Teacher: Yeah...

(3) Student A: You might hear me out I might—you might be able I might be able to change your side or you might be able to affect mine, change it. I just have a problem with that word "universal."

(4) Student B: Well, you can't say all or everything for anything ha ha ha.

(5) Student A: Anything. That's right, ha.

(6) Student B: Take out "universal" and say ah "majority truth" or ha ha...

(7) Student A: Ha...

(8) Student B: Societal...

(9) Student A: You know how much we've gotten off the topic and...

(10) Student B: Ha ha...

(11) Teacher: Well, it is somewhat off the topic because I mean the real topic is whether or not it pays to debate.

(12) Student A: To debate, yeah.

(13) Student B: Debate and whether or not assuming that you were right that all knowledge and all truth is relative to the individual would it pay to hear the other guy's position.

(14) Teacher: That that I think was the question really whether or not to listen or were you wasting your time because you know...

(15) Student A: If you do listen—

(16) Teacher: Uhum

(17) Student A: Maybe I'm just suggesting that for the most part if you do find yourself to have that capital T, that Truth, sometimes you find more than not, the person's already got their mind set and even though they might be hearing you, they're not going to listen to you. They've already established...if they've thought about what they're talking about they've already established it and...

(18) Teacher: One of the points that that they make in this book that...

Consider these sample responses of student interpretations to line (10), "ha ha":

(a) seems sincere
(b) no response given
(c) agreeing
(d) agrees and finds humor
(e) laughter could be out of embarrassment because A had just stated that they had both gotten off the subject
(f) everyone laughs to agree
(g) eases tension
(h) very amiable
(i) likes getting off topic
(j) breaks up the language pattern
(k) joking to move topic along

Sample responses to line (16), "uhum":

(a) not agreement
(b) agreeing to continue conversation
(c) ?
(d) maybe just to acknowledge that the Teacher allowed Student A to cut him off
(e) blank
(f) thinking it over
(g) showing reception

Analysis

With the original speakers present, it is possible both to give them feedback on how people interpret their behavior and for them to give the interpreters feedback on their interpretations. With some good luck, this exercise opens minds to new ideas. The main point for discussion is the varying interpretations that enter into discourse, the rationale that people offer for their interpretations, and the meld of the various interpretations and strategies as people talk. (See Wardhaugh, 1986, especially chapter 4.)

Mental Dynamics

Introduction

One way to divide intrapersonal communication into manageable categories for analysis is to distinguish between what the mind does to stimuli, and how stimuli are represented in the mind. For instance, Posner (1973) organized his masterful textbook on cognition into the statics of cognition (what is in memory) and the dynamics of cognition (what is done to what is in memory, i.e., mental operations). Crowder (1976) dissected the behavioral analysis of the mind into three broad approaches:

(1) stage analysis—the acquisition, retention, and retrieval of information

(2) coding analysis—the aspects of experience that are represented in memory

(3) task analysis—the analysis of skills into subskills.

Think about how you store information in your memory (by statics or coding or mental representations) and how you work on that information in your memory (mental operations). You will begin to get a handle on understanding your own cognitive behavior and that of your students. The following exercise demonstrates some mental operations in the classroom.

Linguistic Intuition: Conscious versus Nonconscious Mental Processing

Goals: This exercise raises for consideration the widely accepted distinction between conscious and nonconscious (or subconscious) levels of thought. While students are generally willing to attribute dreams to the subconscious, and tend to embrace the notion of subliminal perception, they are less familiar with the operations of the nonconscious (or subconscious) in everyday waking activities, such as talking and listening. Recognition of the part that the nonconscious plays in talk is the central goal of this exercise.

Approach: Ask the students to read and respond to each of the sentences below with their judgment of acceptability/unacceptability. Put as simply as possible, the students are to react to each sentence out of their "intuition," or gut response, to its acceptability. Encourage students to respond with as little reflection as possible, and certainly without trying to decide on grammatical rules.

Which of the following sentences would you judge to be ungrammatical (and unacceptable)?

1. Sylvia wanted George to go.
2. Sylvia wanted George go.
3. Sylvia heard George to go.
4. Sylvia hoped George go.
5. Sylvia heard George go.
6. Sylvia looked up the number.
7. Clarence looked the number up.
8. Morris walked up the hill.
9. Morris walked the hill up.

Which of the following sentences seem ambiguous?

10. George wanted the Presidency more than Martha.
11. Ahab wanted the whale more than glory.
12. Visiting professors can be boring.
13. Complaining professors can be boring.
14. The matador fought the bull with courage.
15. The matador fought the bull with swords.
16. They are cooking apples.
17. He killed the woman with a gun.
18. He sat by the bank.

Which of the following sentences would you judge to be unacceptable? The starred sentences are the ones that most people find unacceptable. (See Fromkin & Rodman, 1974, chapter 6.)

1. Sylvia wanted George to go.
*2. Sylvia wanted George go.
*3. Sylvia heard George to go.
*4. Sylvia hoped George go.
5. Sylvia heard George go.
6. Sylvia looked up the number.
7. Clarence looked the number up.
8. Morris walked up the hill.
*9. Morris walked the hill up.

Which of the following sentences seem ambiguous?

10. George wanted the Presidency more than Martha. (structural ambiguity)

    Did George want the Presidency more than Martha did? Or, did George want the Presidency more than he wanted Martha?

11. Ahab wanted the whale more than glory. (structural ambiguity, anomalous)

    Ahab wanted both the whale and glory; but, did glory want anything?

    [People disagree on this one. Native readers see no problem: "glory" would have to be "Glory" for there to be an ambiguity parallel with the George-and-Martha sentence.

Linguists and psycholinguists, on the other hand, say that it is structurally ambiguous because it seems to say, senselessly, that glory wanted something. Teacher, you and your class can chew on this one together.]

12. Visiting professors can be boring.
    (structural ambiguity)

    Is it that visiting in a professor's office can be a bore, or that guest lecturers sometimes numb their hearers?

13. Complaining professors can be boring.
    (not ambiguous)

14. The matador fought the bull with courage.
    (structural ambiguity)

    Did the courageous matador fight the bull, or did the courageous bull fight the matador? (Or both!)

15. The matador fought the bull with swords.
    (structural ambiguity, anomalous)

    Did the matador use swords against the bull, or did the matador encounter a well-armed bull?

16. They are cooking apples.
    (structural ambiguity)

    Is it that we smell some apples cooking? Or, those apples over there, are they for cooking?

17. He killed the woman with a gun.
    (structural ambiguity)

    Did he take a gun and kill the woman, or did he kill her despite the fact that she was the one holding the gun?

18. He sat by the bank.
    (lexical ambiguity)

    Which bank did he sit beside—the river's or the First National?

Analysis

If you are familiar with the linguistics literature, you may recognize these sentences and the underlying principles as coming from various articles and textbooks (for instance, Fromkin & Rodman, 1974; Clark & Clark, 1977; Slobin, 1979). The sentences in this exercise help to show that native language users do have intuitions about their language, and that they seem to have more implicit knowledge about the rules of their language than they are able to make explicit. So, one lesson we gain from this exercise is that native users of the language do have intuitions about the acceptability of sentences.

Moreover, this demonstration makes clear that there is *great agreement* on linguistic intuitions. Given this broad agreement between language users, we have good reason to infer that there must be some base of knowledge that they share. Linguists refer to this base of knowledge as grammar, which comprises syntactic, semantic, phonological, and pragmatic knowledge. Condon (1985) provides a wonderful little introductory textbook for communication studies, integrating the linguist's notion of grammar with the concerns of the student of communication, especially intrapersonal communication.

Because grammar is a rule-based system, it becomes instructive to derive its rules from the implicit (or nonconscious) knowledge that students used in their responses to the exercise. Try some simple theories to account for the regularity of grammatical judgments, for instance, listing parts of speech in each sentence (a sequence of word-types grammar). According to the sequence of word-types grammar, acceptability is determined by an ordered sequence of parts of speech.

When a sequence is found to be acceptable, it predicts *by analogy* other acceptable strings. For instance, sentence 1 predicts that the following sentence is acceptable: Sylvia reminded

27

George to go. Prediction by analogy sometimes works, but sometimes it does not. For instance, 1 incorrectly predicts that 3 will be acceptable, since they are both made up of the same sequence of parts of speech. However, we see that analogy does not predict intuitions about acceptability. Similarly, analogy does little to help in comparing sentences 2, 4, and 5; 3 and 5; but 6 is to 7 as 8 is to 9. Drawing arrows between the sentences to be compared helps make the analogies clear.

Sentences 10 through 18 allow us to consider the nature of intuitions about ambiguity. Class discussion will lead to the conclusion that there is as great agreement here as in acceptability judgments. This part of the exercise raises questions of types of ambiguity:

lexical (18)—river bank or savings bank?

structural (16)—someone is cooking the apples, or those apples are fruit intended for a pie?

semantic (10)—which did George want more, the Presidency or Martha?

pragmatic, i.e., involving anomalous interpretations (15)—did the matador use swords against the bull? Was the bull equally well-armed (and did he fight back)?

Feel free to speculate with your class on how to account for linguistic intuitions.

Biofeedback

Introduction

Biofeedback is the perception of one's own physiological state, often with the aid of instrumentation. Through biofeedback, the individuals are made aware of a physiological state that they were not aware of either prior to the translation of their body's signals into perceptible form, or prior to the attention now being paid to these signals. Typical processes involve heart rate, brain waves, temperature, blood pressure, and muscular tension. An essential component of biofeedback is the individual's ability to alter physiological states upon bringing them to consciousness. Biofeedback is often discussed in textbooks on intrapersonal communication, since it represents a form of "internal conversation." Barker and Edwards (1980) explain that "biofeedback occurs when information about physiological processes of the body is fed back to a person." (p. 44) Two biofeedback demonstrations are described here that are simple and require inexpensive equipment that anyone can use.

Goals: To demonstrate that biofeedback can produce bodily changes and to discuss the intrapersonal communication mechanism that may account for such changes.

Temperature Control

Approach: This demonstration requires a relaxation tape and thermometers. Relaxation tapes are widely available for purchase, whether by mail order or in stores. See advertisements in the Speech Communication Association publications brochure and *Psychology Today*. Ordinary hand-held thermometers will do.

Ask students to hold their thermometers to get a baseline reading of their temperatures. The student continues to hold the thermometer during the relaxation phase. The relaxation tape is played long enough to produce a cooling effect.

Next, while the cooled students are holding the thermometers and are relaxed, encourage them to permit the blood flow to the hands to increase. Tell them to feel an increase in the warmth of the palm. Now, have the students read the temperature registered. This time an increase in their temperature will show.

Relaxation of Muscular Tension

Approach: You can buy a small inexpensive electromyograph machine (EMG) for a few dollars at Radio Shack. Using a simple EMG one student can demonstrate for the rest of the class that it is possible to produce feedback signals reflecting muscular tension, and to change the level of the signal either by lowering or heightening tension. If you lend the EMG instrument to an interested student some days in advance of the demonstration, she or he can experiment with it at home. In the classroom the EMG can be attached very quickly and simply with its Velcro straps (electrodes) which pick up the muscular tension. The EMG reflects the level of muscular tension with a high-pitched sound that all can hear. As the demonstrator relaxes or tenses, an audibly perceptible change occurs in the sound emitted.

Analysis

Most communication teachers are not experts in biofeedback, and that holds true for me as well. But one does not need to be an expert to stimulate discussion and open new areas of interest. My experience has been that it is possible to demonstrate biofeedback in the classroom and to stimulate a great deal of interesting and useful discussion. Often there are people in the class who have encountered some medical problem that responded to biofeedback. Students often will write about biofeedback in their journals. An excellent video that I have used many times is titled, "Biofeedback: Yoga of the West." (See Hartley, 1974.) The video offers a scientific approach to the mind/body relationship highlighted by biofeedback, and helps link the unfamiliar to the familiar.

Depth of Processing

Introduction

How we approach information influences what we get from it. It is one thing to make this claim, and another to demonstrate it. Craik and Lockhart (1972) argue that the way in which we process stimuli is responsible for the persistence of the memory trace. They maintain that we process stimuli in a series of stages, from physical analysis to meaning. The more deeply we process stimuli, i.e., the more we elaborate meaning with associations, images, stories "...on the basis of our past experience..." (p. 675), the more likely we are to remember those stimuli. I speculate further that our interest in the task at hand dictates the degree of attention we pay to stimuli; and, of course, greater interest may reflect greater prior knowledge about the stimuli, i.e., information already in memory.

Depth of processing raises the idea of stages of analysis. (See Crowder, 1976.) A primary aspect of stages of analysis is the difference between structural and semantic analysis. That is, we can focus on the letters, sounds, or syntactic units of words (structural elements), or we can focus on what words mean (semantic component). In this exercise, half of the class is instructed to monitor for structural features, and the other half is instructed to monitor for semantic features. Then an unexpected recognition memory test is given to test for and, predictably, demonstrate that more thoroughly processed, meaningful items are remembered better than merely structural concerns: the students who scan the list for meaning will recognize more of the words than the students who scan the list for structural information.

Goals: The ways we approach, and derive information from, stimuli affects what is stored in memory and, consequently, what is available to memory. This exercise helps to raise for discussion issues in mental dynamics—what we do with what lies in memory. The exercise reinforces the idea that information processing is an active process. Furthermore, it suggests that the mental task influences cognitive behavior and, therefore, cognitive outcomes.

Approach: Half of the class receives the test booklet, which appears below, with the instruction to scan for words containing the letter A. The other half receives the test booklet with the instruction to scan for words that denote a living thing. The instructions appear on the first page of the booklet, so that the student does not know that half the class is performing a different task. Nor are the students aware that they are to be tested for recognition of listed items in the second phase of this demonstration. When all the students have finished the Y/N part of the exercise, distribute the recognition test for the words in the lists they have just scanned. The recognition test is included below, together with the lists for scanning and your list for grading. (See Schulman, 1971; and Craik & Lockhart, 1972 for the procedures used here.)

Depth of Processing Exercise Booklet (Form A)

When the signal to begin is given, turn to the next page where you will find a list of words. Your task is to scan the list of words as quickly as possible, looking for words that contain the letter A. If the word contains an A, then circle the Y next to the word; if not, circle the N. As you complete each page, go on to the next. When you have finished the task, stop and look up to see the time. Write down the elapsed time in order to know how long it took you to complete the task.

Depth of Processing Exercise Booklet (Form B)

When the signal to begin is given, turn to the next page where you will find a list of words. Your task is to scan the list of words as quickly as possible, looking for words that refer to a living thing. If the word refers to a living thing, then circle the Y next to the word; if not, circle the N. As you complete each page, go on to the next. When you have finished the task, stop and look up to see the time. Write down the elapsed time in order to know how long it took you to complete the task.

electrode Y N	warblers Y N	machine Y N
bath Y N	perch Y N	voltage Y N
blanket Y N	scorpion Y N	alphabet Y N
geranium Y N	washer Y N	rubber Y N
frog Y N	top Y N	spend Y N
mussel Y N	crochet Y N	what Y N
termite Y N	engine Y N	wrench Y N
bye Y N	man Y N	thrush Y N
container Y N	camera Y N	honeybee Y N
knitting Y N	goose Y N	kangaroo Y N
shark Y N	vice Y N	drag Y N
railroad Y N	llama Y N	dress Y N
release Y N	lobby Y N	cardinal Y N
hide Y N	numb Y N	entrance Y N
pocket Y N	web Y N	marsupial Y N
gazelle Y N	book Y N	anchor Y N
fat Y N	ant Y N	bring Y N
dolphin Y N	swallow Y N	rude Y N
squirrel Y N	fever Y N	bathtub Y N
pique Y N	now Y N	otter Y N
semicolon Y N	mailbox Y N	osprey Y N
Ohio Y N	ostrich Y N	tennis Y N
brain Y N	hate Y N	want Y N
muskrat Y N	hamster Y N	sort Y N

cylinder Y N	primate Y N	molding Y N
coal Y N	fade Y N	sparrow Y N
lizard Y N	rooster Y N	turkey Y N
gibbon Y N	shutter Y N	robin Y N
trombone Y N	oyster Y N	late Y N
whale Y N	old Y N	calf Y N
lobster Y N	jackal Y N	snake Y N
Manx Y N	sailing Y N	Indiana Y N
brown Y N	cat Y N	cow Y N
exhaust Y N	holder Y N	lose Y N
pizza Y N	department Y N	blackbird Y N
brow Y N	goat Y N	tortoise Y N
chicken Y N	extreme Y N	nail Y N
elephant Y N	journal Y N	horse Y N
name Y N	pill Y N	program Y N
running Y N	koala Y N	Maine Y N
porcupine Y N	alligator Y N	profit Y N
photography Y N	nape Y N	polar bear Y N
service Y N	laughter Y N	fox Y N
shortage Y N	plunger Y N	mile Y N
pheasant Y N	vulture Y N	fish Y N
Connecticut Y N	stork Y N	paint Y N
thermostat Y N	starling Y N	platypus Y N
woodpecker Y N	automobile Y N	lath Y N

Recognition Test

The following lists include some words that were in the lists you just scanned, and some that were not. Please circle the words that you recognize from the lists you scanned.

mouse	mussel
knitting	sewing
music	pocket
canary	swallow
then	now
oat	man
sapsucker	warblers
electrode	spectrum
release	member
gazelle	giraffe
cylinder	semicolon
running	brown
tennis	pill
exhaust	blanket
honeybee	fever
railroad	partition
termite	washer
chicken	turkey
partridge	robin
song	service
Vermont	Connecticut
partisan	pheasant
container	automobile
muskrat	camera
mainstream	radio
dolphin	starling
hide	Indiana
radiant	porcupine
treatise	extract
trash	intern
thermostat	plunger

blackbird	vulture
laughter	confront
alligator	perch
elephant	bye
geranium	holder
top	cat
crochet	ant
pique	brain
bath	Ohio
fox	platypus
demean	dread
fish	scorpion
dream	squirrel
calf	shark
horse	stork
engine	mailbox
lobster	alphabet
wrench	whale
menstrual	bathtub
Manx	oyster
trombone	serpent
marsupial	osprey
square	llama
vice	numb
ostrich	woodpecker
spy	frog
photography	sailing
stick	jackal
guppy	old
sort	dress
bring	theory
spend	web
coal	charm
drag	cardinal
sparrow	dart

entrance	conifer
kangaroo	conflict
otter	primate
fade	voltage
book	crab
what	why
crack	cradle
garbage	rubber
thrush	anchor
rude	lizard
gibbon	machine
rooster	shutter
molding	goat
name	Maine
pizza	gnaw
wing	paint
lath	nail
brow	money
tortoise	polar bear
profit	program
koala	extreme
department	journal
lose	nape
mile	make
snake	cow
late	shortage
goose	hamster
hate	lobby

The starred words (*) appear in the scanning lists. The stars are included here to aid you in scoring, but, of course, do not appear on the students' recognition tests.

mouse	*mussel
*knitting	sewing
music	*pocket
*canary	*swallow
*then	*now
oat	*man
sapsucker	*warblers
*electrode	spectrum
*release	member
*gazelle	giraffe
*cylinder	*semicolon
*running	*brown
*tennis	*pill
*exhaust	*blanket
*honeybee	*fever
*railroad	partition
*termite	*washer
*chicken	*turkey
partridge	*robin
song	*service
Vermont	*Connecticut
partisan	*pheasant
*container	*automobile
*muskrat	*camera
mainstream	radio
*dolphin	*starling
*hide	*Indiana
radiant	*porcupine
treatise	extract
trash	intern
*thermostat	*plunger
*blackbird	*vulture

40

*laughter	confront
*alligator	*perch
*elephant	*bye
*geranium	*holder
*top	*cat
*crochet	*ant
*pique	*brain
*bath	*Ohio
*fox	*platypus
demean	dread
*fish	*scorpion
dream	*squirrel
*calf	*shark
*horse	*stork
*engine	*mailbox
*lobster	*alphabet
*wrench	*whale
menstrual	*bathtub
*Manx	*oyster
*trombone	serpent
*marsupial	*osprey
square	*llama
*vice	*numb
*ostrich	*woodpecker
spy	*frog
*photography	*sailing
stick	*jackal
guppy	*old
*sort	*dress
*bring	theory
*spend	*web
*coal	charm
*drag	*cardinal
*sparrow	dart
*entrance	conifer

*kangaroo	conflict
*otter	*primate
*fade	*voltage
*book	crab
*what	why
crack	cradle
garbage	*rubber
*thrush	*anchor
*rude	*lizard
*gibbon	*machine
*rooster	*shutter
*molding	*goat
*name	*Maine
*pizza	gnaw
wing	*paint
*lath	*nail
*brown	money
*tortoise	*polar bear
*profit	*program
*koala	*extreme
*department	*journal
*lose	*nape
*mile	make
*snake	*cow
*late	*shortage
*goose	*hamster
*hate	*lobby

Analysis

This exercise makes a clear point. It demonstrates empirically that when the students attend to the meaning of a stimulus, as opposed to the physical structure of the stimulus, they are better able to remember and recognize it. What is of real value to the students is the idea that we can process information in different ways, depending upon how we approach the task at hand. This idea reinforces the notion of an active processor, an active communicator. It raises for consideration a host of important theoretical issues. For instance, one may ponder the question: "What is a word?"

This exercise may be viewed as suggesting that a word is a complex, that is, not just one thing with a simple relationship between the word and the referent. The words that make up the stimuli in this exercise are themselves physical objects, with internal structure. They are also symbols that represent a semantic system. In the semantic light, these words are subject to an analysis of their features, such as contrasting features (e.g., animate and inanimate). In addition to the code represented by the word, a cognitive flexibility inheres in each word that allows us to approach it in more than one way. You may wish to note the contexts in which we operate on one or another aspect of a word, e.g., reading a new word for which we do not have a meaning. Or, you may wish to speculate about the implications of depth of processing for listening, learning, displaying involvement, experiencing concentration, and its effects on the individual's state of relaxation.

Reconstruction from Memory: Inference

Introduction

Reconstruction from memory refers to the phenomenon of remembering an experience by reconstructing it from the processed version we have stored. That is to say, we usually do not store a representation of the exact physical stimuli. Instead, we process input into meaning and store that. Upon recall, we remember the meaning we stored, not the stimuli *per se*. That meaning may include inferences that we drew at the time of storage; or, by making use of the wide range of knowledge we have in storage (pragmatics), we may embellish the memory at the time of remembering it.

An interesting and important related issue of practical significance is the "eye-witness report." A demonstration of reconstruction from memory makes one point very clear, namely, that human memory does not work like a tape recorder. As a result, reconstruction from memory undermines in a practical way the common-sense and courtroom notion that an "eye-witness report" is necessarily a reliable report.

For these and other reasons, the idea of reconstruction from memory is enormously important to communication studies. This exercise makes use of sentences taken from various experiments conducted by William Brewer and his associates at the University of Illinois. (See Harris & Brewer, 1973; Bock & Brewer, 1974; Brewer & Harris, 1974; Brewer & Shedletsky, 1974; Brewer & Lichtenstein, 1974, 1975; Brewer, 1975, 1977.)

Goals: This exercise demonstrates that we have a tendency to reconstruct from the original mental stimuli, thereby changing them in various ways. The exercise demonstrates that we make use of syntactic, semantic, and pragmatic knowledge as we transform language. This tendency is so strong that people can even be told in advance that they will alter the input—on average, about 40% of the time in this exercise. This effect is so strong that you can challenge your students to produce nothing but the verbatim items, and then enjoy with them their inability to achieve the task.

Approach: Provide your students with answer booklets for writing their responses. The answer booklet consists of one page for each block of ten sentences. The first few words of each test sentence are shown in the answer booklet. In the sentences listed below, these prompt words are italicized.

Instruct the students to memorize the sentences for exact recall. Present to your class orally the list of forty sentences below, reading them aloud in four blocks of ten sentences each. Read the class a block of ten sentences, and then announce a three-digit number (e.g., 437). After the number is heard, they are to count backwards silently from that number by three's (e.g., 434, 431, 428), and then write the rest of the sentences as they remember them on the back of the answer booklet, where they will not see the prompt words. This number-counting, delay task forces memory of the sentences to shift from immediate memory to long-term memory and assures a reliance on processed input.

After the students have written a few number responses, ask them to turn over the booklet and begin to fill out as many sentences as they can recall. When they have finished, have them turn the booklet face down and listen to the next set of sentences, followed by the number-counting, delay task, and then repeat the process. It is not necessary to use all forty sentences. Any one block of ten sentences will do the job.

Sentence Reconstruction Prompts

1. The bullet...

2. The farmer...

3. The absent-minded professor...

4. The law student...

5. Recorded history...

6. The cat...

7. The student's parents...

8. The four-year-old boy...

9. The hungry python...

10. The paratrooper...

11. The hippo...

12. The Indian...

13. The surfer...

14. The safe-cracker...

15. The St. Bernard...

16. The clumsy chemist...

17. The gold statue...

18. The hi-fi fanatic...

19. Billy Graham...

20. At sunset...

21. The karate champion...

22. The magician...

23. The painting...

24. The girl...

25. The nightgown...

26. The narcotics...

27. Russian...

28. The angry rioter...

29. The voters...

30. Dennis the Menace...

31. All of California...

32. The viper...

33. Several children...

34. The flimsy shelf...

35. The cook...

36. The fireman...

37. The chair...

38. Someone...

39. Miss America...

40. The elephant...

Scoring

Next comes scoring the responses. Your students will likely express some uncertainty during the scoring, and decisions will need to be made. What counts as correct? Do we count, for instance, *can't* the same as *cannot*? Scoring will certainly prompt discussion, a good point at which to explain that one of the main purposes of the demonstration is to compare verbatim recall to recall for meaning or gist. To score responses in class, distribute a handout showing the presentation sentences. Also, list the following four scoring categories with their definitions:

(1) An "Exact" is an absolutely identical reproduction of the original.

(2) An "Omission" is an instance of a total lack of written response.

(3) An "Error" is any response that changes the meaning of a sentence.

(4) A "Shift" is a change in form without a change in meaning. (A "pragmatic implication," defined below, forms an exception—the relationship between pragmatically related sentences is based on world knowledge rather than on semantics.)

A Shift occurs when a word is changed to its synonym, but the sentence maintains its original meaning. ["The nightgown was too little (small)."] Alternatively, a Shift occurs when one or more words are deleted or relocated without changing the meaning of the original sentence. ["The cat jumped over the wall and the dog jumped over (it) too." Or, a change from "Tarzan heard the jungle drums at sunset" to "At sunset Tarzan heard the jungle drums."]

A pragmatic implication (P.I.) is also considered a Shift. P.I. refers to a sentence that is implied by another sentence but which does not necessarily follow. (See Brewer, 1977.) For instance, "The hungry python caught the mouse" pragmatically implies that "The hungry python ate the mouse." Such responses are scored as Shifts.

You may wish to assign the task of developing a scoring system. Since judgment calls are required, and joint decisions need to be made, it is instructive to score at least some sentences with class participation. Exacts, Omissions, and Errors are straightforward; they simply require following the category definitions precisely, whereas Shifts require judgment. Part of the enjoyment of this exercise is negotiating Shift scores with your students. This demonstration is great fun, astonishing in its effects, and always works.

Test Sentences: The test sentences are taken from the studies by Brewer cited in the bibliography. The italicized words are used as prompt words in the students' prompt booklets.

The shift types indicated are defined as follows:

Synonym = synonym or substitution.

Syntax = one or more words are deleted or relocated, i.e., a change in form without a change in meaning.

P.I. = pragmatic implication, refers to a sentence that is implied by another sentence but that is not necessarily true.

Deixis = words that "must be interpreted in relation to the particular time, place, person or discourse context of the sentence." (Brewer & Harris, 1974, p. 321.)

L.I. = logical implication, refers to "those semantic relationships where one sentence seems to be necessarily implied by another." (Brewer, 1977, p. 673.)

1. *The bullet* struck the bull's-eye.
   Synonym, e.g., hit

2. *The farmer* plowed the field but the farmer did not fertilize the field.
   Syntax, e.g., fertilize it

3. *The absent-minded professor* didn't have his car keys.
   P.I., e.g., forgot, lost

4. *The law student* had passed the bar exam.
   Deixis, e.g., student passed

5. *Recorded history* started thousands of years ago.
   Synonym, e.g., began

6. *The cat* jumped over the wall and the dog jumped over it too.
   Syntax, e.g., over too

7. *The student's parents* sent bail money to him.
   Syntax, e.g., him bail money

8. *The four-year-old boy* struck the golf ball.
   Synonym, e.g., hit

9. *The hungry python* caught the mouse.
   P.I., e.g., ate

10. *The paratrooper* leaped out the door.
    P.I., e.g., jumped out the plane

11. *The hippo* frightened the children.
    Synonym, e.g., scared

12. *The Indian* was hiding below the bridge.
    Synonym, e.g., under, beneath

13. *The surfer* almost lost his swimming suit.
    Synonym, e.g., bathing suit, trunks

14. *The safe-cracker* put the match to the fuse.
    P.I., e.g., lit

15. *The St. Bernard* was too large for the car.
    Synonym, e.g., big

16. *The clumsy chemist* had acid on his coat.
    P.I., e.g., spilled

17. *The gold statue* was in the center of the square.
    Synonym, e.g., middle

18. *The hi-fi fanatic* turned the volume up.
    Syntax, e.g., turned up

19. *Billy Graham* told a dirty joke to the President.
    Syntax, e.g., President a dirty joke

20. *At sunset* the jungle drums were heard by Tarzan.
    Syntax, e.g., Tarzan heard the jungle drums at sunset

21. *The karate champion* hit the cinder block.
    P.I., e.g., broke the cinder block

22. *The magician* touched the girl and the girl disappeared.
    Syntax, e.g., she

23. *The painting* that the gallery sold was a forgery.
    Syntax, e.g., painting the gallery

24. *The girl* selected a platinum ring.
    Synonym, e.g., chose

25. *The nightgown* was too little.
    Synonym, e.g., small

26. *The narcotics officer* pushed the doorbell.
    P.I., e.g., rang

27. *Russian* language is difficult to pronounce.
    Synonym, e.g., hard

28. *The angry rioter* threw the rock at the window.
    P.I., e.g., a rock through the window

29. *The voters* received what they deserved.
    Synonym, e.g., got

30. *Dennis the Menace* sat in Santa's chair and asked for an elephant.
    P.I., e.g., lap

31. *All of California* had felt the earthquake.
    Deixis, e.g., California felt

32. *The viper* threw itself on her.
    Synonym, e.g., jumped at

33. *Several children* amused themselves.
    Synonym, e.g., played

34. *The flimsy shelf* weakened under the weight of the books.
    P.I., e.g., collapsed

35. *The cook* was fired and the janitor too.
    Syntax, e.g., was fired too

36. *The fireman* sprayed water on the fire.
    P.I., e.g., put out

37. *The chair* is on top of the box and the box is to the right of the tree.
    L.I., e.g., the chair is to the right of the tree

38. *Someone* dropped the delicate glass pitcher.
    P.I., e.g., broke

39. *Miss America* said that she played the tuba.
    P.I., e.g., played the tuba

40. *The elephant* has been eating more than the hippo has been eating.
    Syntax, e.g., the hippo has

Analysis

This exercise makes a point very convincingly: we distort in non-random ways when we remember sentences. Obviously, this demonstration holds important implications for psychology and for the nature of memory, as well as for intrapersonal communication. It provides us with a reminder that the receiver plays an active role in the communication process, that information is not merely sent and received as water is flushed through a conduit, or even as an electronic message is sent from modem to modem. Instead, the receiver takes an active part. Knowledge already stored in memory and the new knowledge that gets stored in memory are both relevant to the process of receiving communication. The interplay between current stimuli and stored knowledge is relevant to the process of interpretation. This exercise, in short, validates empirically what is meant when we say that meaning is not in the word; meaning is in the person.

Active versus Passive Processing

Introduction

Some theorists have discussed the passive/active distinction as the difference between those times when we know something because "it looks right" to us, even though we do not "know" why, and those times when we know something because we have worked at figuring out a pattern or rule that we can state. Active processing of input produces qualitatively different results in learning compared to passive processing. The "Depth of Processing" exercise (p. 31) makes clear that what goes on during processing (e.g., structural versus semantic analysis) affects the outcome. Similarly, active processing may be thought of as a form of problem-solving in which incoming stimuli are related to knowledge in memory. During active processing, the person may be relating incoming stimuli to stored meanings or concepts, verbal or nonverbal: The mind may be formulating hypotheses that concern the attributes of incoming stimuli, e.g., patterns or rules underlying a sequence of stimuli. That is, the person who is actively processing is working on making sense out of the experience.

The distinction between active and passive processing is a key issue in intrapersonal communication. One way to provide students with a clear understanding of the distinction between active and passive processing is to show that the two forms of processing lead to very different outcomes in retrieval from memory. The following exercise makes this difference evident in concrete terms.

Goal: The goal of this exercise is to show that active processing produces a very different result from passive processing: Active processing empowers the learner.

Approach: Half of the class is given Form A, and the other half is given Form B. Each form is self-explanatory.

Active versus Passive Processing (Form A)

Instructions

Take several seconds to examine list A. Try to figure out a pattern or a rule that describes the sequence.

List A: 1 2 3 4 5 6

Next, take several seconds to examine list B. Try to find a pattern or a rule that describes it.

List B: 1 4 7 10 13 16

Finally, take several seconds to examine list C. Then try to write it down on the reverse side of this sheet.

List C: 2 4 8 16 32 64 128 256

Active versus Passive Processing (Form B)

Instructions

Take several seconds to examine list A. Memorize list A and write it from memory on the reverse side of this sheet.

List A: **7 1 4 8 3 9**

Next, take several seconds to examine list B. Memorize list B and write it on the reverse side of this sheet.

List B: **6 3 5 7 0 2 8**

Finally, take several seconds to examine and memorize list C. Write list C from memory on the reverse side of this sheet.

List C: **6 4 5 2 6 4 2 6 3 1 1 8 2 8 2**

Analysis and Scoring

The responses can be scored quickly and easily in class. Only list C need be scored. Take the number of correct digits for each student, beginning with the first, and terminate the count at the first error. This will produce an overall count of how many digits each student was able to reproduce. If the scores are listed on the chalkboard by group (Forms A and B), you will have an overall count of the total number of digits produced with each processing style.

You may observe that the two lists C, while containing identical numbers, are quite different. Whereas list C on Form A is sequential, ordered, and some numbers are grouped, list C on Form B is random. Clearly, Form A will produce different results from form B. Form A, given its tendency to encourage active processing (i.e., the use of underlying rules to describe the sequences) will produce significantly greater ability to reproduce the patterns. Form B, given its tendency to emphasize passive and rote memory, is liable to produce a limited ability to retrieve list items. The difference in outcome between the two lists should open some discussion on the difference between passive versus active processing.

Concept Formation

Introduction

The human ability to abstract ideas, and thereby form concepts, is inseparable from what and how we communicate. This is true whether we are thinking about how we attribute traits/states to people (including one's own self-concept) and events, labelling, or reducing uncertainty (Berger & Bradac, 1982) or relating symbols to reality. (Condon, 1985) As with active and passive processing, concept formation may be thought of in terms of problem solving. When the problem to be solved is how to organize and make sense of behavior, we can see how concept formation is a form of intrapersonal communication.

The idea that the receiver parses behavior has been referred to as "the punctuation of the sequence of events." (See Watzlawick, Beavin, & Jackson, 1967.) For instance, when we decide that someone is a certain kind of person (e.g., smart) or in a certain state (e.g., happy), or when we decide on the structure of an event (e.g., that one communicator initiated an argument), we have made use of concept formation. In the same way, recognition of context and the internal connections within the text may be viewed as a form of problem-solving that relies on concept formation. (Halliday, 1970) The concept of concept formation is an infinitely rich source of ideas and relationships for communication theory. The following exercises raise the topic of concept formation for initial inspection.

(1) Concept Identification: Physical Attributes

Goals: To have students experience forming concepts. The students will have an opportunity to look inward as they attempt to form a concept. They will see that the active process of concept formation involves abstracting, selecting attributes, and testing hypotheses.

Approach: Tell the class that you will be showing them a set of geometric figures, one per page. Each visual either is or is not an example of a concept that you have written down out of the students' view. The students' task is to decide whether or not each visual represents the concept that you have written down. (You write it down so that you can't cheat.) After viewing each visual, the students silently guess whether or not that figure is in fact an example of the concept you have written down; and you then tell them whether or not that figure is in fact an example of the concept: "Yes, it is," or "No, it is not." Every so often, as you are going through the visuals, you may wish to ask for a show of hands on how many think the last one is an example of the concept, and how many think it is not. After you complete showing all the visuals, ask the class to indicate what the concept is. The sequence in which you show the visuals to the class is as follows:

Visual	*Is the visual an example of the concept?*
(1) large uncolored triangle	No, it is not.
(2) large uncolored circle	Yes, it is.
(3) large uncolored square	No, it is not.
(4) small uncolored circle	No, it is not.
(5) small uncolored triangle	No, it is not.
(6) large colored circle	Yes, it is.
(7) small colored triangle	No, it is not.
(8) large colored circle	Yes, it is.
(9) small colored square	No, it is not.
(10) small uncolored circle	No, it is not.

The concept that you have written down is "large circle."

Materials

The materials consist of a sequence of simple geometric figures, one per page. Throughout the sequence, each figure occurs in two sizes, large and small (e.g., the large square is roughly 4 1/2" x 4 1/2" and the small square is roughly 2" x 2").

The exact sizes of your large and small figures do not matter, so long as the large ones are noticeably larger than the small ones, and both types are consistent in size throughout. The figures are drawn in two styles—a simple outline and a colored-in version. The exact color does not matter, nor is it critical whether or not you maintain consistency in color choices.

Procedure

Show the class a visual. Give them a chance to guess silently whether or not it is an example of the concept that you have written down. Provide your feedback: "Yes, it is," or "No, it is not."

As the students are taking in the information of which they are required to make some sense (i.e., stimuli among which they must find some order or pattern), they are abstracting and formulating a concept through which they can organize seemingly diverse data by pointing to their commonality. At sight of the first visual, there is of course absolutely no way that the students can make an intelligent guess. So, you simply get started, and the task becomes clear after a few pictures. To make it more of a challenge, do not allow the students to write down either their guesses or your feedback.

Analysis

The concept which you wrote down and which defines the pattern of your feedback is "large circle." It takes into account three physical dimensions: size, color, and shape. By abstracting these physical dimensions into concepts, and by making use of the feedback, the students, by testing whether each diagram is an instance of the concept, can discover through a process of exclusive logic the concept "large circle" that you have written down.

Some students will, I predict, reason their way to the solution. It may help them to let them know that the concept is simple and not tricky. It is also useful to take a vote by show of hands at various points in the exercise to let everyone know that there is agreement on the yes/no guesses, even before they know what the answer is.

For instance, by turn (4), most people will guess "yes." It is interesting to speculate why this is: perhaps we develop and test hypotheses as we actively process stimuli towards identifying a concept. Since the attribute "circular" had met with a "yes" response earlier, the students may be hypothesizing at this point that the concept is "round things." Part of the problem then is to decide which attributes are relevant and which are irrelevant—a central issue in concept identification.

Another interesting point is that some people may develop a hypothesis that works for several turns, only to prove wrong in final analysis. When a hypothesis works for a while and then proves wrong, it may be difficult for the individual to reconstruct the original stimuli and the feedback. Such an eventuality may lead to useful discussion of how people sometimes find themselves in a similar state of confusion in, for example, the interpersonal world of human relations. Another line of discussion to pursue is that our failed hypotheses often force us to unlearn our concepts and formulate new ones.

(2) Concept Identification: Semantic Attributes

Introduction

Concept formation, when viewed as a process of abstraction, is the recognition of commonality among diverse stimuli. That is, the instances of a concept may differ in many ways but be perceived as similar or identical with regard to some one attribute or few attributes. In the previous exercise we saw how physical attributes might be used to form a concept. The following three exercises demonstrate that abstracting a concept from a collection of instances may proceed along semantic lines, i.e., making use of symbols and meanings.

Goal: The goal of this exercise is to demonstrate that we are influenced in concept formation by the meaning we attribute to symbols.

Approach: These three exercises deal with symbols. The first exercise is taken from Cofer (1954, 1965). It shows that we organize input in memory and that at least one way to organize input is by attending to meaning. Items that are similar in meaning, or that cluster together under a concept, are likely to be organized under that concept. Items early in a list tend to activate certain attributes and thereby set the stage for what follows. This suggests that we do organize input according to its meaning.

Concept Identification: Meaning (a)

Instruction

Present students with the following list of words. After each word, they are to guess silently whether or not that word is an instance of a concept which you have written down out of their view. Following each stimulus word, pause to give students time to guess at the concept; then give the class your feedback, "yes" or "no," indicating whether or not that item is an instance of the concept in question. The concept for which they are searching the list is "things powered by electricity." This exercise resembles the previous "large circle" exercise, except that here the concept to be identified is semantic rather than physical and visual.

Stimulus Item	Is the stimulus item an example of the concept?
stereo speaker	yes
aspirin	no
photograph	no
sailboat	no
traffic sign	no
sun	no
stop sign	no
candle	no
air conditioner	yes
subway	yes
television	yes
stereo	yes
bicycle	no
window fan	yes
toaster	yes
match	no
foot	no
hair dryer	yes
computer	yes
slide rule	no
traffic light	yes
tape recorder	yes
electric chair	yes
bookcase	no

Analysis

This exercise brings to light that some concepts are built up out of semantic features. We are alerted to the distinction between concepts that are based on the physical features of the stimulus item, and concepts that are based on the meaning of the stimulus item. The list used in this exercise is challenging, since a number of potential concepts are liable to be considered, such as "human-made devices" or "things that humans benefit from." Again, the main point made by this exercise is simply that we make use of the meaning of words in forming concepts.

Concept Identification: Meaning (b)

Instructions

Tell the students that they will hear a list of four words. Their job is simply to decide as fast as possible, and with as little thinking as possible, which word does not fit with the others, and write it down.

Stimulus List
1) Prayer Temple Cathedral Skyscraper
2) Put Pot Pan Spoon
3) Hog Root Soil Carrot
4) Tennis Baseball Football Beachball
5) Ocean Dunes Sand Desert

Analysis

This exercise is very effective at demonstrating that we have alternative ways of organizing a body of data, in this case a list of words. When students are asked to respond quickly to these lists, to select the first word that comes to mind, they consistently offer a concept exemplified by either the first word in the list or the last. The great majority consistently produces the concept exemplified by the first word in the list. What is suggested by this demonstration is that we do have a subjective mental dictionary, of sorts: Words (or concepts) are organized mentally, and when we register a word, it activates related words. A kind of mental readiness to receive and organize seems to occur.

Concept Identification: Syntax/Meaning

Introduction

This exercise is playful and simply reinforces the others. It depends on the way English usage represents the plural in a variety of forms. The concept to be identified is "plural."

Instructions

Run this exercise in the same way as the previous exercises, presenting the students with a stimulus item followed by feedback, "yes" or "no," the feedback to indicate whether or not the stimulus item is an example of the concept. The students must guess at whether or not the stimulus item is an example of the concept, until they can identify the concept.

Stimulus Item	*An example of the concept?*
hat	no
deer	yes
toe	no
dogs	yes
cat	no
sheep	yes
foxes	yes
farm	no
category	no
moon	no
men	yes
female	no
children	yes
cup	no
elephant	no
dish	no
feathers	yes
race	no
brought	no
flames	yes

Self-Concept

Introduction

The idea of self-concept fits so well with the exercises just described that we would be missing an opportunity not to consider self-concept here. The foregoing exercises help to bring home the meaning of the concept "concept." For me, at least, the notion of self-concept takes on more meaning and new meaning when I recognize that it refers to a human-made construct having the main feature of any other concept, namely, that self-concept is an abstraction. That is to say, in the context of concept formation, we recognize that self-concept is a construction of our own making, based on diverse bits of abstraction that we ourselves select.

Goal: The goal of this exercise is to point out that self-concept is built up out of abstractions and concepts. The processes of abstraction, selection, and hypothesis-testing apply here as much as they do in the other exercises on concept formation.

Approach: The exercises suggested here are not new ones; they are found in fuller form in various texts. (See Strause & Ambrester, 1986, pp. 16-17; Roberts, Edwards, & Barker, 1987, pp. 111-112; Goss, 1989, p. 84.) I mention them here in brief form to offer a suggestion about concept formation.

Instructions

(1) Ask the students to write a short list of 10 to 20 words that describe themselves, words that respond to the question: "Who am I?"

(2) Next, ask the students to decide how they *feel* about each word in their list. Do they like it? Dislike it? Have no strong feelings about it either way? How do they think a "significant other" would rate each of the words? The students enjoy

doing the last part of the exercise by trying a variety of significant others.

Analysis

Forming a concept and forming a self-concept are similar processes. Explore this similarity with your students by discussing the following questions: How do I make abstractions about myself? How do I identify concept patterns that hold true about myself? How do I test hypotheses about my self-concept? Is it hard to change a hypothesis about myself when it proves wrong?

Suggest that your class characterize the listed items selected for their self-concept. That is, have them notice the sorts of concepts that are used to describe the self. Do we describe ourselves by listing roles we play, and if so, what sorts of roles? Do we make reference to our work? To our appearance? Name? Personality?

Suggest that they compare their own lists with the speculative lists that they imagined their significant others might make for them: Do I see myself as (I imagine) others see me? It is interesting to make a comparison between lists, i.e., how we and our significant others compare in valuing the various features we have selected for ourselves and imagine that they have selected. (See Greene & Geddes, 1988, for an interdisciplinary communication/cognitive science study of how self-concept is represented mentally, how retrieval processes operate on stored self-knowledge, and how the cognitive model of the self-system relates to action.)

Analysis of Verbal Codes

Introduction

Coding analysis raises the fundamental question: What is it that gets learned? (See Crowder, 1976, chapter 1.) That is to say, what aspects or features of a stimulus are involved in the learning process and in what is retained? Coding analysis is a focus on how a stimulus is represented in memory. It concerns the attributes that play a role in retention and retrieval.

The following exercises show that we employ various codes in representing our experiences to ourselves, and that these make a difference in how we retain and retrieve information. Moreover, the way that the stimulus comes into us does not necessarily determine the code by which the stimulus is represented internally. In other words, recoding, or transformation of input, occurs.

Phonological Coding in Immediate Memory

Goal: The goal of this exercise is to show that the mode of stimulus presentation does not necessarily define the code for internal representation.

Approach: This exercise mimics a milestone study performed by Conrad (1964), in which subjects were presented with brief exposures to arrays of consonant letters. Each trial consists of a brief exposure to a sequence of six consonant letters visually displayed. The student's task is to take in the display silently and, without any intervening activity, to recall the display in order after it has disappeared. Ask the students to write down their responses.

Materials

Present the following four sequences printed large enough for the whole class to see. Hold up each sequence long enough for the students to read it once, silently—about the amount of time it takes you to say 1001 to yourself.

(1)   B H K T C V

(2)   B C T H V Z

(3)   H B K L M W

(4)   G F N L X H

Analysis

A look at errors in recall demonstrates the nature of the internal code used for representing the visual letter stimuli. The crucial data in this demonstration is the nature of the errors. Substitution errors, i.e., when the correct letter for a given position is replaced with an incorrect letter, do not seem to be random. Substitution errors tend to consist of replacing the correct letter with another letter similar in sound. For instance, the letter V is likely to be replaced by the letter E, since the two letters rhyme.

Furthermore, sequences that have a high proportion of rhyming letters—(2) above—are harder to recall than sequences with few or no rhyming letters—(3) above. Under classroom conditions, this demonstration produces approximately five times more substitution errors with sequences (1), (2), and (4) than with sequence (3). These findings have led to the conclusion that immediate memory is closely tied to the hearing-speech (phonological) system. (However, no claim is made that the phonological system is the only code possibly in use here.)

Visual versus Verbal Coding

The "Depth of Processing" exercise (p. 31) demonstrates the influence of semantic versus structural coding on retrieval. The speed and accuracy associated with visual versus verbal coding is demonstrated with the following exercise that mimics a study carried out by Coltheart, Hull, and Slater (1975). Subjects were asked to scan the alphabet mentally from beginning to end, determining letters with the sound "ee" in one task, and, in a second task, determining letters with a curved shape. Since being correct about the sounds is independent of visualizing the letters, and since correctly judging the shape of the letter is independent of the letter's name, the hypothesis was that these tasks reflect purely verbal and purely visual processing, respectively.

Goal: The goal of this exercise is to bring attention to subtle differences in cognitive operations between superficially similar tasks. The exercise causes us to see that cognitive operations may vary in significant ways between tasks. In addition, this exercise invites students to experience a set of tasks from a published experiment, so that they may gain some understanding of how theoretical conclusions are reached.

Approach: The approach is to replicate, with some modification, experimental procedures taken from Coltheart, Hull, and Slater (1975).

Instructions

Say to your students: "When I say 'start,' mentally scan the alphabet from A to Z, and count the number of letters with the long "ee" sound, as in the letter E. Do this as quickly as possible, since I am timing you. When you have done it, put up your hand, so that I will know when the last person is finished. Write down the number you count, and don't change it!"

After the group completes this first task, move to the second. Ask them to scan the alphabet mentally from A to Z as fast as possible, counting the number of letters with a curved shape. They are to raise their hands when finished, since they are being timed.

The correct answer to the sound "ee" exercise is 9, and the correct number of letters in the alphabet with a curved shape is 11.

Analysis

It is not necessary actually to time the exercises. The appearance of timing the class is used to make people do the task as fast as they can (while still trying to be accurate). There is, however, a predictable effect to be observed on the basis of timing: it takes more time for people to perform the visual task than the auditory one.

After the original research, Coltheart, Hull, and Slater reported a sex difference in the results. Females proved more accurate on the verbal task, and males more accurate on the visual. Others, myself included, have failed to replicate this finding. Your demonstration will turn up interesting results that may lead to class debate. As for representational systems—the codes for representing stimuli mentally—discussion of the participants' experiences in the two tasks is in order.

Finally, these scanning tasks open discussion about "task analysis," i.e., the idea that we can analyze tasks as consisting of constituent cognitive behaviors. For instance, we may speculate that scanning the alphabet for curves requires more steps than scanning the alphabet for sounds. The visual task may require both naming the letters during scanning to bring each to mind, and visually scanning each to determine shape. The verbal task may not require the extra step of visualizing.

Important here is the idea of decomposing tasks into subskills. Clearly, such an analysis holds value for the psychology of representing information in the mind. But it also holds value for intrapersonal communication because it raises for consideration the idea that the process of communication could break down at various points, that an individual's ability to interact may depend upon numerous processes, and that individuals may differ in their ability to carry out a subroutine. As a result, people may have preferences and individual styles for interacting with their environment.

Individual Differences

Introduction

It is both intuitively appealing and scientifically accurate to recognize the existence of a wide range of individual differences in cognitive performance. Perhaps one of the benefits of classroom discussion of intrapersonal communication is to learn that we have much in common and, at the same time, that we each have our own unique style of intrapersonal processing. Moreover, a healthy respect for individual differences is entirely compatible with understanding the nature of social-scientific methodology. Although scientific results are based on statistical summaries, individual differences must not be ignored. The following exercises focus on individual differences.

Goals: These exercises demonstrate that individual differences exist, and raise for discussion the implications of individual differences for communication.

Approach: Each of the following two exercises is a fairly simple measure of cognitive behavior. The "Cognitive Style" exercise is a self-report aimed at assessing the degree to which an individual is a verbalizer or a visualizer. The "Direction of Gaze" exercise measures eye movement while a person is initiating reflective thought. In teams of two, one teammate answers reflective questions, while the other takes note of the direction of the answerer's gaze. (See Richardson, 1977.)

Cognitive Style

The scoring is designed to be performed quickly and easily. In the roughest way, it distinguishes verbalizers from visualizers. The individual's score is computed simply by adding up the scores on all fifteen items. Verbalizers will score high (10-15), visualizers will score low (0-5), and mixed verbalizers-visualizers will score in the middle. To calculate, simply attribute the following values to the T and F responses:

1. T=1 F=0
2. T=0 F=1
3. T=1 F=0
4. T=1 F=0
5. T=0 F=1
6. T=1 F=0
7. T=0 F=1
8. T=1 F=0
9. T=1 F=0
10. T=1 F=0
11. T=0 F=1
12. T=1 F=0
13. T=1 F=0
14. T=0 F=1
15. T=0 F=1

Cognitive Style

Circle your response (True or False) to each statement:

1. I enjoy doing work that requires the use of words. T F
2. My daydreams are sometimes so vivid, I feel as though I actually experience the scene. T F
3. I enjoy learning new words. T F
4. I can easily think of synonyms for words. T F
5. My powers of imagination are higher than average. T F
6. I seldom dream. T F
7. I read rather slowly. T F
8. I cannot generate a mental picture of a friend's face when I close my eyes. T F
9. I believe that people cannot think in terms of mental pictures. T F
10. I prefer to read instructions about how to do something rather than have someone show me. T F
11. My dreams are extremely vivid. T F
12. I have better than average fluency in using words. T F
13. My daydreams are rather indistinct and hazy. T F
14. I spend very little time attempting to increase my vocabulary. T F
15. My thinking often consists of mental pictures or images. T F

Direction of Gaze

Instructions

Pair off the students. One member of each pair, the interviewer, asks the questions shown below, and the other answers. The interviewer is to note the partner's direction of gaze while the partner answers, and to circle the direction of gaze as the response data (right, left, up, down, straight, or eyes closed). The direction of gaze is the first direction towards which the eyes look immediately after the question has been asked. Instruct the interviewer not to inform the answerer that direction of gaze is being recorded. When all ten questions have been asked, the interviewer can tabulate the number of left versus right eye-movements. In preparation for discussion, the percentage of left versus right eye-movements may be calculated. The interviewer also writes down the interviewee's answers, both because this would be expected and to keep a record of the number of correct answers. Before beginning the questions, the interviewer is to find out from the answerer the additional information required in the exercise questionnaire:

Direction of Gaze Exercise

Before you ask the questions, find out the following information from your partner:

MALE/FEMALE

RIGHT-HANDED/LEFT-HANDED

NATIVE ENGLISH SPEAKER

LEFT-HANDED RELATIVES

Note your partner's direction of gaze without letting him or her know that you are observing which way the eyes move first after the question has been asked.

R = right   D = down
L = left   S = straight
U = up   EC = eyes closed

Also, write down your partner's answer to each question.

The Questions

1. Tell me on which side the President parts his hair.

   R L U D S EC

   RESPONSE:

2. Think about this proverb and interpret its meaning for me: "Better a bad peace than a good war."

   R L U D S EC

   RESPONSE:

3. How many letters are there in the word "anthropology?"

   R L U D S EC

   RESPONSE:

4. Think of a circle drawn so that it cuts each side of a square in two places. Into how many parts is the square divided by the circle?

R L U D S EC

RESPONSE:

5. Tell me an English word that starts with "L" and ends with "C."

R L U D S EC

RESPONSE:

6. Think of a clock face. The time is 10 past 10. Now imagine the clock turned towards a mirror. Ten minutes later you look into the mirror. What time does it appear to be?

R L U D S EC

RESPONSE:

7. Give me the answer to the following arithmetic problem: 125 divided by 5 and multiplied by 4.

R L U D S EC

RESPONSE:

8. Try to recall what your bathroom sink looked like when you got up this morning. Describe it to me.

R L U D S EC

RESPONSE:

9. Imagine seeing yourself climbing a steep hill. When you reach the top, tell me what you see.

R L U D S EC

RESPONSE:

10. Give me the answer to the following multiplication problem: 126 multiplied by 5.

R L U D S EC

RESPONSE:

This demonstration is doable in the classroom, easy to score on the spot, and useful in raising for consideration the idea of brain organization, cognitive style, and individual and sex differences.

Analysis

Neuroscience describes the relationship between the brain's organization for information processing and the movement of the eyes during reflective thought. (See Bakan, 1969; Kinsbourne, 1972, 1974; Richardson, 1977.) When the eyes move to the right, the left hemisphere is active; when the eyes move to the left, the right hemisphere is active. Based on the idea that the left hemisphere is the seat of verbal processing, and that the right hemisphere is the seat of visual processing, some researchers hypothesize that verbal questions (such as questions 2, 3, 5, 7, and 10) tend to produce eye-movement to the right, whereas visual questions (such as questions 1, 4, 6, 8, and 9) tend to produce eye-movement to the left. However, the correlation between direction of gaze and type of question (verbal or visual) has not held up consistently. What has emerged, though, is the finding that individuals show a consistency in direction of gaze during reflective thought, independent of the type of task at hand. (See Bakan, 1969; and others.)

Some evidence suggests that direction of gaze is related to the subject's family history of handedness, i.e., whether or not the subject has a left-handed parent or sibling. (See Levy, 1976.) That is why the "Direction of Gaze" questionnaire asks if the subject has a left-handed relative. You may wish to explore the relationship between the student's handedness, family handedness, and direction of gaze.

Some researchers have reported sex differences in direction of eye-movement during problem solving; but again, this finding has not proved reliable. To repeat, the consistent finding here is that each individual tends to look either right or left during problem solving.

Using the ten-item questionnaire presented in the "Direction of Gaze" exercise, Richardson (1977) categorized subjects who moved their eyes eight or more times in one direction as right-movers or left-movers. The great majority of subjects fell into either one or the other category, right- or left-movers. Richardson further tested his subjects on their cognitive styles, categorizing them into verbalizers or visualizers. (See the "Cognitive Style" exercise, p. 77.) He then correlated habitual direction of gaze with cognitive style and found strong correlations, although these turn out not to be reliable in some studies. There is a correlation between direction of gaze and cognitive style, but it is likely related to additional variables that we do not fully understand yet.

Some researchers have proposed that direction of gaze is related to the sex of the subject. It has been supposed that females would tend to look right and males left, based on the idea that females have a propensity for using their verbal left hemisphere, and males for using their spatial right hemisphere. In my studies I have found the opposite to be true: females tend to look left and males tend to look right.

Huang and Byrne (1978), testing all female subjects, found that right movers tended to be narrow categorizers, who are thought to be analytic in cognitive style; and left-movers and mixed-movers tended to be broad categorizers, thought to be holistic in cognitive style. Again, there seems to be reason to believe that there is a strong connection between cognitive style and direction of gaze, although the relationship is likely to be mediated by other variables, such as the sex of the subject.

Ideal Self-Description

Goals: This exercise raises questions about sex differences, individual differences, and sexual stereotypes; it replicates procedures used by Block (1973).

Approach: The following questionnaire aids in discovery of one's "ideal self."

My Ideal Self-Description

The list below contains words that could describe a person. As you read down the list, ask yourself, "Out of all these characteristics, what kind of person would I most want to be?" Circle any 16 of the 32 descriptions that best state what kind of person you would want to be; you are not required to circle one from each pair. You may circle any 16 descriptions out of all 32 that you choose, but only 16.

1. Adventurous
2. Considerate
3. Independent
4. Cheerful
5. Fair, just
6. Idealistic
7. Responsible
8. Helpful
9. Sense of Humor
10. Talkative
11. Self-centered
12. Uncertain, indecisive
13. Moody
14. Curious
15. Feels guilty
16. Artistic

1. Ambitious
2. Reserved, shy
3. Rational, reasonable
4. Sensitive
5. Self-controlled
6. Perceptive, aware
7. Critical
8. Vital, active
9. Competitive
10. Generous
11. Dominating
12. Sympathetic
13. Assertive
14. Impulsive
15. Practical, shrewd
16. Loving, affectionate

Scoring

Place a letter "M" next to both number ones, a letter "F" next to both number twos, an "M" next to both number threes, and so on, alternating down the list. Add up the total number of m's, giving each item the value 1. Add up the total number of F's, giving each item the value 1. Subtract the smaller number from the larger. A high score in the "M" direction indicates that the student shows a preference similar to the males in the original study; a high score in the "F" direction indicates that the student shows a preference similar to the females in the original study. Compare the mean score of the males to the mean score of the females.

In the following lists, * indicates items on which males in 1973 scored significantly higher, and ** indicates items on which females in 1973 scored significantly higher; a = agency, c = communion, n = neutral (explained below).

Sexual stereotypes may have changed since 1973. To see how similarly your subjects compare to the United States subjects in the original study, count the number of females and males who selected each item, rank the 8 most numerous male choices and the 9 most numerous female choices, and compare with the lists below.

Male Stereotypes
Practical, shrewd*a
Assertive*a
Dominating*a
Competitive*a
Critical*a
Self-controlled*n
Rational, reasonable*a
Ambitious*a
Feels guilty n
Moody n

Female Stereotypes
Loving, affectionate**c
Impulsive**n
Sympathetic**c
Generous**c
Vital, active**a
Perceptive, aware**n
Sensitive**c
Reserved, shy**n
Artistic**c
Curious n

Self-centered a   Uncertain, indecisive n
Sense of Humor n   Talkative n
Responsible n   Helpful c
Fair, just n   Idealistic n
Independent a   Cheerful n
Adventurous a   Considerate c

Analysis

The Ideal Self-Description exercise is an attempt to compare males and females in terms of the concepts they use to identify themselves. Block (1973) built this comparison on the basis of Bakan's distinction between "agency" and "communion." (Bakan, 1966) Block explains: "Agency is concerned with the organism as an individual and manifests itself in self-protection and self-expansion. Communion, according to Bakan, is descriptive of the individual organism as it exists in some larger organism of which it is a part and manifests itself in the sense of being at one with other organisms." (p. 515)

Block was studying stereotypes, not prescribing behavior; but her results, perceived as normative for the U.S.A. in 1973, led her to the conclusion that agency and communion are contrasting principles of socialization for girls and boys, and that the results of that socialization tend to show up in adult self-definitions. Using these terms with reference to the table above, all the items on which males scored higher than females were in the category of agency or were neutral; all of the items on which females scored higher than males were, except for one (Vital, active), in the category of communion or were neutral.

This exercise will surely stir up in your class the never-ending discussion of the differences between males and females. In terms of your class, have the stereotypes changed since 1973, or are they still pretty much the same?

Social Cognition

Introduction

By social cognition I mean both social and cognitive behavior. Roloff and Berger defined social cognition broadly as the way people think about people (1982, p. 10). Social cognition involves thought processes focused on people and their behaviors, as opposed to thought about inanimate objects. Whereas other persons are the usual target of social cognition, one's own self can also be a legitimate target of social cognition. Under this broad conceptual umbrella we find research on anticipating counterarguments; parsing the sequence of events; constructing generalizations about the self, about others, and about actions. We find research on expectations, attribution, impression formation, cognitive balance, self-concept, attention, self-monitoring, attitude, belief, intention, explanation of social phenomena, and more. Some of the exercises earlier in this book could also come under the heading of social cognition. "Self Concept," "Group Discussion," and "The Journal," for instance, could all be viewed as exercises in social cognition.

The approach here is to offer an exercise allowing the class to produce and analyze utterances that reflect a complex underlying body of knowledge relating to how people behave, including cause-and-effect assumptions, beliefs about reality, norms concerning responsibility, rights, obligations, values, priorities, morality, duty, and—generally speaking—all cultural knowledge. The way we think about other people may teach us something about how we think about ourselves, just as the way we think about ourselves teaches us about how we think about others.

Accounts

Goal: The goal of this exercise is to demonstrate that in ordinary talk we use a rich and organized body of knowledge about how people behave.

Approach: Ask each member of the class to think of a hypothetical, but realistic, "account" that one person might offer either internally or to another in explanation of something that happened, and why. Admitting that this instruction is vague, get volunteered examples from the class without biasing the type of account by offering one or two examples yourself. Once one member of the class is willing to offer an account, the others will find it easy to follow suit. Each brief account is written on the chalkboard, without any analysis at first. Typical accounts are: (1) "I would have come sooner but my car was broken." (2) "I didn't do well on the test because I wasn't feeling well." (3) "I skipped class today because I wanted to."

After all the accounts have been written on the board, ask the class to read them, seeking generalizations that can be made about them. The students are to treat the accounts as data and look for patterns. Typically, the students will mention some of the key ideas presented by Scott and Lyman (1968) in their seminal article titled, "Accounts." Some of these are: responsibility for action; good and bad behavior; intentionality; priorities; locus of control, within the person or external to the person.

Analysis

Drawing on student input, let the discussion lead to some key concepts (e.g., responsibility for one's behavior, appeals to forces outside of one's control, good and bad behavior). One of the most attention-getting distinctions to be made is the one between accounts that acknowledge wrongdoing but reject responsibility [examples (1) and (2), above] and accounts that deny wrongdoing (i.e., assert that the behavior in question is good) and accept responsibility [example (3) above]. Scott and Lyman refer to these types as excuses and justifications, respectively. Once the distinction between excuses and justifications has been drawn, let the class go through the accounts on the board, labelling each as either an excuse or a justification. Fuzzy cases may not fit neatly into either category, but will open lively debate.

Part II

A Reflection on the Mind at Work

> Communication is not governed by fixed social rules; it is a two-step process in which the speaker first takes in stimuli from the outside environment, evaluating and selecting from among them in the light of his own cultural background, personal history, and what he knows about his interlocutors. He then decides on the norms that apply to the situation at hand. These norms determine the speaker's selection from among the communicative options available for encoding his intent.
>
> (Gumperz and Hymes, 1986)

This book on intrapersonal communication is about the part our minds play in communication—our perceptions, memories, experiences, feelings, interpretations, inferences, evaluations, attitudes, opinions, ideas, strategies, images, and states of consciousness. This book is designed to help students examine their thought processes, since thought and communication are inseparable. As students learn more about the subconscious and self-reflective mind, its representations, operations, and products, they will acquire a greater understanding of, and greater control over, their communication behavior. The central goal of intrapersonal communication theory is to increase awareness, understanding, and choice.

In teaching about intrapersonal communication, I have found that students are very willing to explore their own minds in furthering their understanding of communication. This willingness on their part to undertake self-observation is what makes the exercises in this book so effective. You will find, as I have found, that by facilitating the students' self-awareness of intrapersonal communication, you succeed in deepening their understanding of communication, and, at the same time, you help them improve their communication skills. In my experience, college students at any age are eager both to explore their intrapersonal communication and to communicate about themselves with others. They are also eager to speculate about intrapersonal processes. When the classroom atmosphere is noncoercive and open to exploration, students quickly find that they have interesting and curious experiences to offer, and that they are not alone in the human experience. The students become their own laboratory experiments as they begin to look inward at intrapersonal communication.

A Sampler of Definitions

The term intrapersonal communication is not used frequently in communication literature. A search of *Communication Abstracts* over the decade of the 1980s shows a scarcity of references to intrapersonal communication. Recently published textbooks on communication, however, show a growing awareness of the cognitive perspective, whether or not they explicitly use the term "intrapersonal." (See, among others, Littlejohn, 1983; Barker, 1987; Fisher, 1987; Reardon, 1987.) A few textbooks on intrapersonal communication have appeared in the past few years.

Some theorists say that intrapersonal communication is about communication with one's self, that is, the talking that goes on inside one's head. (Barker & Edwards, 1980; Weaver & Cotrell, 1985) According to this view, intrapersonal communication takes place when the sender and the receiver are the same person. Vinson (1985) presents a closely related definition. According to Vinson, intrapersonal communication "...is the sending and receiving of messages within the human organism. The structure or processing subsystems which comprise ITC [intrapersonal communication] are neurophysiological in nature." (p. 2) Bode defines intrapersonal communication as "...inner speech that occurs during moments of selective deep caring which is self or other directed." (1985, p. 1) (For more on inner speech, see Korba, 1987.) For Biddle, intrapersonal communication is the way "I bring about a union of the disparate parts or potentially separated parts of my being." (1985, p. 2) LaFleur discusses intrapersonal communication in terms of "the ways in which persons interpret (decode) the multiple potential meanings of both internally and externally originating sentences and sentence fragments." (1985, p. 1) Barker and Kibler, discussing a conceptual overview of communication, define intrapersonal communication this way:

> *Intrapersonal Communication* is the basic level from which all other forms of human communication are derived. It is that communication which occurs within the individual. It involves the evaluating of and reacting to internal stimuli. These evaluative and reactive processes help human beings to cope with and understand ideas, events, objects, and experiences. Thinking is one form of intrapersonal communication. (1971, p. 4)

Ruesch and Bateson discuss intrapersonal communication as a level of communication characterized by both proprioception (reception from within) and exteroception (reception from external stimuli); both propriotransmission (internal transmission of messages) and exterotransmission (external transmission of messages); and the central functions of coordination, interpretation, and storage of information (1968, pp. 276-279). Roloff and Berger liken intrapersonal communication to social cognition: both are characterized as internal processing; both involve representational systems; both are focused on self, others, and behaviors; and both are assumed to have some impact on behavior. (1982, pp. 24-26)

In a critique of the concept "intrapersonal communication," Cunningham (1985) provides an extensive and organized list of functions and properties attributed to intrapersonal communication. (Also, see Cunningham, 1989.) Moreover, he challenges the theoretical soundness of many of those ideas that have gone into defining intrapersonal communication. Underlying Cunningham's arguments is the claim that communication typically entails the features of community, message (meaningful/informative), and transfer or sharing of the message. It is chiefly the first feature, community, that accounts for the bulk of his concern. Can we speak of communication when we limit our definition to the individual, the single person, one organism only? In short, Cunningham says no, because either (1) we are back to the shaky metaphysical status of attributing psychological faculties to the person in the "talking to oneself" perspective, or (2) we stray from the idea of communication as being about community, society—more than one person. Cunningham wrote:

> In a field that undertakes to instruct us about the central fundament of community and society, IaC [intrapersonal communication] pulls us in the opposite direction by postulating a very private and opaque process that is said to be or to comprise [parts of] the individual psyche. (1985, pp. 25-26)

Cunningham raises a second concern and in so doing lays the groundwork for important and difficult theoretical decisions, namely, the question of the atomic versus the discursive nature of cognition and intrapersonal communication. That is to ask, do all mental structures and operations comprise intrapersonal communication, or just some? Or, to put the question in other words, where up the cognitive ladder, from mental elements to high-level mental constructions, does intrapersonal communication begin to occur?

The question of exactly when communication has occurred is a problem for all levels of communication, and has been widely debated. I attempt no answer to that question here, but that should not deter us from exploring intrapersonal communication: academic studies are replete with central concepts that evade unitary definition. Our fuzziness on what life is, does not keep us from studying biology. Our confusion over what language is, does not deter us from linguistics.

Intrapersonal Communication Is More Than Just Talking to Yourself

Contrary to some of the definitions mentioned above, I argue that intrapersonal communication is more than communication only with one's self, as that phrase is ordinarily understood. (See Roberts, 1983; Halfond, 1985; Roberts, Edwards, & Barker, 1987.) Intrapersonal communication is a level of communication not defined by the number of people involved, the communicative functions served, or the channels of communication used. Intrapersonal communication consists of mental processes that operate every time we communicate. The exercises in this book allow one to explore intrapersonal communication involving all the mental processes that provide the mind with its experiences; one's view of one's self and the world; one's feelings, thoughts, strategies, reasons, motivations, knowledge, and states of consciousness. (See Goss, 1982.)

Intrapersonal communication is about the individual's processing of stimuli, both verbal and nonverbal. Sometimes those stimuli are generated within the perceiver, and sometimes they are received from outside the perceiver. Sometimes what is generated remains within the individual (e.g., talking with one's self, "seeing" images, or having physiological sensations), and sometimes what is generated is expressed (e.g., speech and gesture).

The study of intrapersonal communication is also, therefore, the study of decoding and encoding—the study of meaning-making. Whether or not what is decoded originates inside or outside the body of the intrapersonal communicator, and whether or not what is encoded is actually expressed, leaked, or given off, intrapersonal communication has occurred. (See Goffman, 1959.) Stated broadly, intrapersonal communication is about the relationship between the individual and the stimuli that the individual encounters.

Without engaging in a lengthy theoretical debate, I would like to address a handful of nagging questions that are being discussed regarding intrapersonal communication.

Foremost among these questions are two: (1) the "disciplinary" question—Does not cognitive psychology already study intrapersonal communication? How does intrapersonal communication differ from related disciplines, especially cognitive psychology, linguistics, and philosophy? (2) the question about "community"—How many people are needed to communicate? Are not at least two people needed to communicate?

The disciplinary question can be approached on a number of grounds: political and territorial, historical, methodological, and theoretical. In a discipline characterized by its interdisciplinary nature at every level, and by its admittedly weak definition of itself as a separate entity, the "how does it differ?" question is always a hard one. If one is really asking, "Who has the right to ownership of the discipline?" then the question may translate, "Who was here first?" But chronology does not resolve the question of which discipline should be working on a problem. Many disciplines share roots; new disciplines often have emerged from earlier ones, notably, psychology from philosophy, linguistics from anthropology, and speech communication from speech. The critical issue is theory, not ownership.

Without an adequate theoretical response to the question of where intrapersonal communication belongs, we are in no position to place it in its proper discipline. On what basis can we judge whether it really belongs in cognitive psychology or in linguistics or in communication? In the end, an area of study finds its home where the theory and methodology of a discipline require it. Unlike cognitive psychology, intrapersonal communication is not concerned with thought *per se*, or with mental dynamics *per se*. Unlike linguistics (and its related areas, e.g., discourse analysis, pragmatics), intrapersonal communication is not interested in cognitive content for its part in accounting for linguistic intuitions *per se*. Instead, intrapersonal communication is interested in cognition—knowledge, cognitive structure, feelings, etc.—for its part in the act of communicating.

In a special issue of the *Journal of Communication,* titled "Ferment in the Field," a number of prominent scholars wrote about the definitional and disciplinary issues of the field of communication. (See the *Journal of Communication,* Summer 1983, Volume 33, No. 3.) Reference to intrapersonal variables occur throughout that volume, although the authors are likely to be discussing social and policy aspects of communication research. Miller, for instance, wrote:

> This respect for the individual's role in his or her own behavior is largely responsible for the emergence of rule-following rather than law-governed conceptions of communications. To a lesser extent, it buttresses the argument that an actor's perceptions of or meanings for a given situation constitute the primary data for communication researchers—a position advocated, among others, by the constructivists. Volitional action, rather than causally shaped motion, is seen by these scholars as the generative mechanism for symbolic exchange. (1983, p. 32)

Research on communication effects leads us back to the individual and to the conceptual underpinnings of our ways of thinking about ourselves. This takes us to the question of the individual versus society: Can we talk about communication within the individual? Behind this question lies the assumed dichotomy of the individual and society. We are often led to think that we can speak of one or the other. But the definition of intrapersonal communication proposed in this book does not allow us to isolate the individual from society.

In our intrapersonal focus on the individual, let us not confuse the distinction between internal versus external stimuli with the theoretical difference between the individual and society. Study of intrapersonal communication is, in fact, the investigation of the interface between the individual and the social-cultural environment. Billig, Condor, Edwards, Gane, Middleton, and Radley make the point well:

> We see thinking as inherently social. In fact, thinking is frequently a form of dialogue within the individual. (See Billig, 1987.) Yet the content of the dialogue has historical and ideological roots, for the concepts involved, and their meanings, are constructed through the history of social dialogue and debate. In this sense the social pattern of ideology is mapped onto individual consciousness. Similarly, because of its dilemmatic nature, ideology cannot preclude thought and debate. Thus, the paradox of "the thinking society" describes the reality that our dilemmas of ideology are social dilemmas and that our ideology cannot but produce dilemmas to think about. (1988, pp. 6-7)

When we speak of the individual engaged in intrapersonal communication, this should not be interpreted as severing the individual from the community. We are simply focusing on that part of the process of communication that takes place intrapersonally—the individual's encoding and decoding of messages.

Clearly, the definition of intrapersonal communication is controversial; but this should come as no surprise. After all, the elements that enter into intrapersonal communication—the self, communication, mind, meaning, information, and consciousness—are all complex and controversial. I offer you my definitions of communication, meaning, and mind. In the end, you will decide which definitions of intrapersonal communication fit with your models of communication.

Intrapersonal Communication Is at the Center of All Communication

In describing the field of communication, Fisher (1987) pictures "a nested hierarchy of communication systems." (p. 3) As one can see in Fisher's diagram, intrapersonal communication

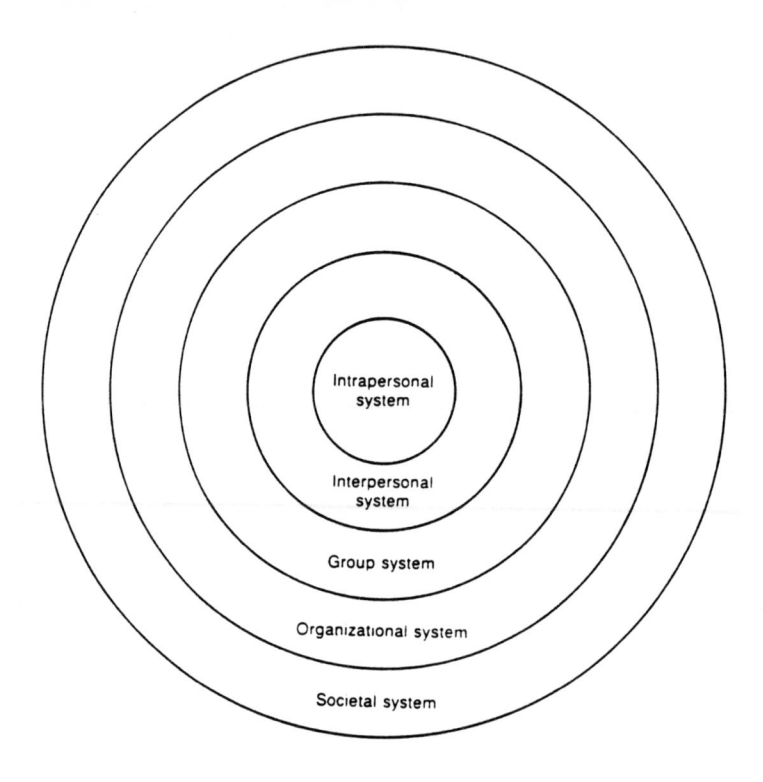

Nested Hierarchy of Communication Systems

is at the center of concentric circles, with interpersonal, group, organizational, and societal systems surrounding it. This imagery is helpful. It helps to remind us that, while we may speak of separate levels of communication—and we may build courses around these levels, we are dealing with interrelated components of an individual self situated in its society. Each system in the diagram affects and is affected by the other systems.

What is "communication"? Students in my introductory course on communication regularly offer these key ideas on day one: sending, conveying, transmitting, exchanging messages between two or more people. These typical and popular ways of conceptualizing the communication process are summarized in what Lakoff and Johnson (1980) label as the conduit metaphor. According to the conduit metaphor, words are thought of as containers of meaning. When we communicate, we send messages from one place to another like water sloshing through a conduit. The word is the conduit carrying the meaning to its destination.

Lakoff and Johnson, however, reject this idea of language and communication, because it implies that meanings are the objective properties of words rather than the subjective products of interpretation. The conduit metaphor holds no room for the role that context plays in interpretation. It suggests that the literal meanings of words are what we communicate to one another. Moreover, the conduit metaphor suggests that communication of ideas is something that happens to the receiver. What comes out at the end of the conduit is what the receiver gets—according to the conduit metaphor, the receiver is passive before the incoming stimuli in reception of the message.

Lakoff and Johnson say that the conduit metaphor reflects the common-sense way of thinking both about language and communication and about the nature of meaning. When we talk about communicating through language, we tend to emphasize the function of conveying literal meaning (or what has been variously called factual, propositional, representative, ideational, and descriptive meaning). But, of course, we also communicate other kinds of information when we talk, and we do this without expressing that information literally. For instance, we communicate how we regard the person we are talking to, our group identity (social class, native region, etc.), whether or not we want to be having this conversation, what our role and/or communication relationship is in relation to the person with whom we are interacting, and much, much more. (See the "Who's Afraid of Virginia Woolf?" exercise, p. 6.)

You could think of this type of meaning as interpersonal meaning. It has been variously called social expressive, relational, and emotive information. The ways in which we communicate literal meaning and interpersonal meaning are different from one another, though they are both forms of communication. Is it possible to define "communication" so as to include both literal and interpersonal meanings? Is it also possible then to define "intrapersonal communication" as focusing on this inclusive understanding of meaning?

Everyone knows that communication is an active process. What does this mean? Where do the dynamics of communication reside? How do they work? Both old information (in memory) and new information (received) are subject to the dynamics of mental processing. Stimuli take on meaning in context. The "recognition of information" requires knowledge on the part of the receiver, even if that knowledge is only knowledge of the literal meaning of words. Communication is thus interactive—both the receiver (the knower) and the thing known (object, word, action, and sender) are taken into account. Clearly, this interactive model of communication includes more than does the conduit metaphor.

What does "the recognition of information" mean? "Recognition" is the use of stored knowledge in the memory by which we perceive (make sense of) stimuli. In other words, recognition requires a "going to" the mental "storehouse" and there retrieving knowledge for use in decoding sensations from the outside. When you recognize a word on this page, you make use of your stored knowledge of written English. When I use the term "information," I mean anything that has meaning for the receiver. This information is not necessarily interesting, significant, or new. Only when we categorize things and events do they become meaningful. (See the first "Silence" exercise, p.13.) Some examples of information are: common names of objects like "car" and "bicycle"; categories of events like greetings, invitations, suggestions, news, descriptions (Austin, 1962; Searle, 1969); and indications that something is, was, or will be. Communication occurs when we—verbally or nonverbally, consciously or nonconsciously—categorize. In other words, communication occurs when we have an idea, when we assign meaning. This view of communication is a cognitive perspective—it focuses on the mental activity of transforming sensations into meaning. This leads us to a working definition of intrapersonal communication.

A Receiver-Based Definition of Intrapersonal Communication

Intrapersonal communication concerns the processes of assigning meaning (e.g., the mental structures and the retrieval processes of memory) and the products of assigned meaning (e.g., schemata, labels, and memories—or more generally, representations).

This view of communication places emphasis on the interpreter (the receiver). No interactant is required—you may "just" get an idea on your own, no interlocutor needed. Nothing is implied about the intentions of a sender or the source of stimuli, the type of stimuli (verbal or nonverbal), the relationship between the stimuli and the idea or feeling, or the level of consciousness of either the sender or receiver. Accordingly, when you look out on a clear blue sky and feel uplifted, you have experienced communication. When you think, as you walk along, "I've got to get the laundry done," you have experienced communication. When you have a conversation with another person, exchanging both literal and interpersonal meanings, read a book, or watch television, you have experienced communication. What all of these experiences have in common is that the receiving mind has processed stimuli, interpreted the stimuli, and mediated a response. For none of the above is an observable response required. That is, the receiver may respond to the meaning he/she attributes to the event, and that response may not be observable.

I define communication as broadly as possible to include all instances of symbolic thought. (See Cronkhite, 1986.) But even if one limits communication (as some researchers do) to its prototypical case, i.e., intended messages between two people having a face-to-face conversation, my main point applies: the information processing of intrapersonal communication is centrally involved in the communication event. Limited by the narrower definition of communication, one may overlook that part of the communication process is deciding whether or not messages have been produced and sent, and whether or not they were intended. Recognition of an incoming message is part of the information being processed—communication is what we, as receivers, figure out. (Worth & Gross, 1974; Messaris & Gross, 1977) It is precisely this "what we figure out" that this book is all about.

Assigning Meaning

Consider for a moment what would happen if we could not recognize messages, determine their literal and their interpersonal meanings. One-on-one, prototypical communication could not take place. Clearly, the ability to assign meaning is prerequisite to the prototypical case. This takes us back to the idea that communication does not happen to us passively—we actively do it. We interpret and categorize what we encounter (see the "Group Discussion" exercise, p. 19). We assign meaning to words, deeds, events, and objects (see the "Concept Formation" exercise, p. 61). To learn more about communication, then, we need to understand how we assign meaning. That is the main purpose of this book: to explore how our minds work when we interpret.

Philosophers have pondered the nature of meaning for at least as long as the history of Western philosophy. More recently, linguists have worked intensively to describe the meaning in a word, and how words combine to form sentence meaning. (For a review of linguistic semantics, see Raskin, 1983.) Publication of linguistic research on meaning and language use—the ways in which actual utterances signal meaning to people in social context—is relatively recent. (Levinson, 1983)

"Context" may be thought of as all the many ways in which utterances (and nonverbal behaviors as well) gain meaning from a surrounding frame of reference—e.g., physical objects, discourse, long-term and short-term memory, mutual knowledge, public (cultural) and private (interpersonal) knowledge, and so on. Clearly, the construction of context is itself an intrapersonal act. Many researchers use the term "semantics" to refer to meaning derived from hypothetically constructed (i.e., context-free) sentences, and the term "pragmatics" to refer to meaning derived from utterances in context. Semantics (that part of linguistics concerned with literal meaning) and pragmatics (roughly, the meanings of utterances in context) are linguistic topics alive with controversy, and that includes their interrelationship. Semantics and pragmatics, nevertheless, are sources of many insights that increase our understanding of how we communicate.

One of the most important insights for communication theory is the idea of *types* of meaning. We gain far more information from what people say than merely the literal meanings of the words or sentences they utter. Consider the sentence:

Do you know the Barley Mow?

The Barley Mow is a pub in Brighton, England. With that information filled in, you can give some literal meaning to the sentence. Perhaps you simply interpret it as: *Are you familiar with a certain pub called Barley Mow?* And if this is the reading you give the sentence, then you also interpret it as a question—it is punctuated with a question mark. Literally, it is a question requiring a yes/no answer. But you can see that in context it is much more than a yes/no question. All kinds of other questions arise: Who would ask you such a question? What do they have in mind? Where are they going with this line of questioning? Do they have any expectations about your answer? Are they referring to the night of the brawl? Do they know that you left before the fight broke out and long before the police arrived? How you interpret the question depends greatly on the context in which you receive it.

Consider this context: You are an American male visiting in Brighton, England. You and your eight-month-old baby step into a restaurant, and get into a conversation with a British man, who also has a baby. You mention that you enjoy the pubs and that you go to one called The Golden Cannon, with which, as it turns out, your interlocutor is familiar. At this point in the conversational context, he utters the sentence: "Do you know the Barley Mow?"

Now, how do you interpret the sentence? The question, as you may have surmised, is leading to something more—"Do you know the Barley Mow? You ought to try it. It's near The Golden Cannon. Come around on Sunday at noon and I'll be there playing darts. Join me!" You are relieved that the line of questioning was not leading to a subpoena, but to a pleasant evening at the pub. It is quite usual to ask a question as a prelude to offering an invitation or making a request. (Labov & Fanshel, 1977; Stubbs, 1983)

The main point that I want to make is twofold:

(1) Context is crucial to the interpretive process—context is itself part of the information that we use in interpreting utterances and events. Communication occurs *in context*.

(2) We glean far more from an utterance in context than merely its literal meaning. This second point reinforces our grasp of the layers or levels or *types* of meaning, an idea crucial to communication theory.

We have already encountered two types of meaning, literal meaning and meaning in context. We recognize the meaning or function of an utterance both in the stream of talk (to ask a question, to show agreement) as well as in the social encounter (to be friendly, or distant, or polite, or in some other way to define the relationship). We use information provided by a context to interpret utterances made in the context, and we ourselves supply background information to the context of communication.

Mind as Information Processor

The concept of mind: I think it is important to acknowledge that mind is a "something" that none of us has ever encountered directly with our senses. None of us has seen a mind, tripped over one, or even heard one. The same holds true for "communication" and "meaning." Nevertheless, it is entirely natural for us to speak of our minds as objects—something we can lose, make up, change, or be "out of." You might say that language, through its ability to name concepts, and to fix nonthings as things, misleads us to assume that the abstract concept "mind" stands for something like a chair, a thing that we can sense directly.

As I use the word, "mind" is a convenient short-hand term for referring to our enormous ability to process information. Consistent with this, "mind," as I use the term, is what transforms stimuli into meaning. The mind figures out both the literal meaning and the meaning in context. (Clark & Lucy, 1975; Glucksberg, Gildea, & Bookin, 1982; Schweller, Brewer, & Dahl, 1976) The mind is thus "the instrument" that operates on stimuli to formulate contexts and recognize events in context. Mind produces interpretations.

Fortunately, a great amount of research has been done in psychology and linguistics that gives us some idea of how our mental apparatus transforms sounds and visual images into meaning. This transformation of meaningless sensations into structures of meaning (information) is what we call information processing.

A handful of main points about information processing can be stated: (1) The mind operates at high speed. (2) The mind has a very limited workspace for processing immediate, current stimuli. (3) The mind employs stored knowledge when transforming stimuli into meaning. (4) The mind operates simultaneously or nearly simultaneously (we are not certain which) on various layers of meaning—it recognizes sounds, images, tactile stimuli, words, phrases, sentences, utterances, relations between utterances and larger chunks of discourse, literal meaning, implied meaning(s), the speaker's intended meaning, the function of what was said (e.g., to ask a question, to give advice, to make a statement), the hearer's attitude toward the message and its speaker, the appropriateness or inappropriateness of what was said, its ambiguities, vagueness, hints, degree of politeness, sincerity, and likelihood of being true—*all* "at once."

While it is tempting to think that we build up from smaller units (like sounds) to larger units (like phrases), it is clear that context (i.e., a larger unit) also influences how we process smaller units. Most likely, there is a dynamic interplay among the layers of knowledge. Normally, all of this occurs without our conscious effort or awareness of the interpretive process. Posner distinguishes between effortful and effortless search, which amounts to a way in which experimental cognitive psychology can talk about states of consciousness. Posner explains:

> Effortless retrieval occurs when the input contacts its address in memory without any conscious search. Effortful retrieval occurs when the subject is forced to search the items retrieved into active memory, or when he does not have sufficient content to locate the items in long-term memory unambiguously.
> (1973, p. 43; see also, Shedletsky, 1989)

When we examine the interpretive process, we are to a great extent studying the subconscious mind. People are not able to tell you reliably and precisely what their minds do while in the process of determining meaning. Yet, we react to ourselves, to one another, and to the environment on the basis of our minds' interpretations. The exercises in this book are designed to bring to the student's attention the cognitive behaviors that ordinarily go unnoticed. By raising components of the intrapersonal process to consciousness, we may understand them better and may even be able to make conscious choices in their use.

Intrapersonal communication processes are essential to the communication event. In order to understand how we communicate, we need to understand how we derive meaning through our intrapersonal communication processes. We need to consider our reactions to meanings, our emotional triggers (see Steil, Barker, & Watson, 1983, pp. 94-102), our cognitive style, storage systems, mental dynamics, and representations. We need to consider how we think as we communicate. We need to consider meaning itself, and how the mind constructs meaning. We need to acknowledge the various "types of meaning" that we draw from utterances, and that types of meaning is a significant feature in linguistic communication. Literal meaning, meaning derived from context, and the functional meaning of an utterance (e.g., to invite, maintain contact, request) are among the types of meaning. Use of these exercises will enable you and your students to increase your understanding of the many dimensions of this complex process, and to take greater control over your own intrapersonal communication.

References

Albee, E. (1962). *Who's afraid of Virginia Woolf?* New York: Pocket Book.

Austin, J. (1962). *How to do things with words.* New York: Oxford University Press.

Bakan, D. (1966). *The duality of human existence.* Chicago: Rand McNally.

Bakan, P. (1969). Hypnotizability, laterality of eye movement and functional brain asymmetry. *Perceptual and Motor Skills, 28(1),* 927-932.

Barker, L. (1987). *Communication* (4th ed.). Englewood Cliffs, NJ: Prentice-Hall.

Barker, L., & Edwards, R. (1980). *Intrapersonal communication.* Dubuque, IA: Gorsuch Scarisbrick.

Barker, L., & Kibler, R. (Eds.). (1971). *Speech communication behavior: Perspectives and principles.* Englewood Cliffs, NJ: Prentice-Hall.

Bensen, H. (1975). *The relaxation response.* New York: Morrow.

Berger, C., & Bradac, J. (1982). *Language and social knowledge.* London: Edward Arnold.

Biddle, P. (1985, November). *Intra-self communication.* Paper presented at a meeting of the Speech Communication Association, Denver, CO.

Billig, M., Condor, S., Edwards, D., Gane, M., Middleton, D., & Radley, A. (1988). *Ideological dilemmas.* Beverly Hills, CA: Sage.

Block, J. (1973). Conceptions of sex role: Some cross cultural and longitudinal perspectives. *American Psychologist, 28(6),* 512-526.

Bock, K., & Brewer, W. (1974). Reconstructive recall in sentences with alternative surface structures. *Journal of Experimental Psychology, 103(5),* 837-843.

Bode, R. (1985, November). *Does secular humanism inhibit intrapersonal inquiry?* Paper presented at a meeting of the Speech Communication Association, Denver, CO.

Brewer, W. (1975). Memory for ideas: Synonym substitution. *Memory and Cognition, 3*(4), 458-464.

Brewer, W. (1977). Memory for the pragmatic implications of sentences. *Memory and Cognition, 5*(6), 673-678.

Brewer, W., & Harris, R. (1974). Memory for deictic elements in sentences. *Journal of Verbal Learning and Verbal Behavior, 13*(4), 321-327.

Brewer, W., & Lichtenstein, E. (1974). Memory for marked semantic features versus memory for meaning. *Journal of Verbal Learning and Verbal Behavior, 13*(2), 172-180.

Brewer, W., & Lichtenstein, E. (1975). Recall of logical and pragmatic implications in sentences with dichotomous and continuous antonyms. *Memory and Cognition, 3*(3), 315-318.

Brewer, W., & Shedletsky, L. (1974). *Reconstructive recall: Verb-phrase deletion and pronominalization.* Unpublished manuscript, University of Illinois, Champaign-Urbana.

Brown, G., & Yule, G. (1983). *Discourse analysis.* Cambridge: Cambridge University Press.

Clark, H., & Clark, E. (1977). *Psychology and language: An introduction to psycholinguistics.* New York: Harcourt Brace Jovanovich.

Clark, H. & Lucy, P. (1975). Understanding what is meant from what is said: A study in conversationally conveyed requests. *Journal of Verbal Learning and Verbal Behavior, 14*(1), 56-72.

Cofer, C. (1954, April). *The role of language in human problem solving.* Paper presented at the Conference on Human Problem Solving Behavior, New York University, New York.

Cofer, C. (1965). On some factors in the organizational characteristics of free recall. *American Psychologist, 20*(4), 261-272.

Coltheart, M., Hull, E., & Slater, D. (1975). Sex differences in imagery and reading. *Nature, 253*(5491), *438-440.*

Condon, J., Jr. (1985). *Semantics and communication* (3rd ed.) New York: Macmillan.

Conrad, R. (1964). Acoustic confusions in immediate memory. *British Journal of Psychology, 55*(1), 75-84.

Craig, R., & Tracy, K. (Eds.). (1983). *Conversational coherence*. Beverly Hills, CA: Sage.

Craik, F., & Lockhart, R. (1972). Levels of processing: A framework for memory research. *Journal of Verbal Learning and Verbal Behavior, 11*(6), 671-684.

Crawford, L. (1989). Silence and intrapersonal observation as an initial experience. *Speech Communication Teacher, 3*(2), 11-12.

Cronkhite, G. (1986). On the focus, scope, and coherence of the study of human symbolic activity. *The Quarterly Journal of Speech, 72*(3), 231-246.

Crowder, R. (1976). *Principles of learning and memory*. Hillsdale, NJ: Lawrence Erlbaum.

Crowder, R. (1982). *The psychology of reading*. New York: Oxford University Press.

Cunningham, S. (1985, November). *Intrapersonal communication: A critique*. Paper presented at a meeting of the Speech Communication Association, Denver, CO.

Cunningham, S. (1989). Defining intrapersonal communication. In C. Roberts & K. Watson (Eds.), *Intrapersonal communication: Original essays* (pp. 82-94). New Orleans, LA: Spectra.

Dauw, D. (1980). *Increasing your self-esteem*. Prospect Heights, IL: Waveland Press.

Edwards, R., Honeycutt, J., & Zagacki, K. (1988). Imagined interaction as an element of social cognition. *Western Journal of Speech Communication, 52*(1), 23-45.

Fisher, B. (1987). *Interpersonal communication: Pragmatics of human relationships*. New York: Random House.

Fromkin, V., & Rodman, R. (1974). *An introduction to language*. New York: Holt, Rinehart and Winston.

Glucksberg, S., Gildea, P., & Bookin, H. (1982). On understanding nonliteral speech: Can people ignore metaphors? *Journal of Verbal Learning and Verbal Behavior, 21*(1), 85-98.

Goffman, E. (1959). *Presentation of self in everyday life*. New York: Doubleday/Anchor Books.

Goss, B. (1982). *Processing communication: Information processing in intrapersonal communication.* Belmont, CA: Wadsworth Publishing Company.

Goss, B. (1989). *The psychology of human communication.* Prospect Heights, IL: Waveland Press.

Greene, J., & Geddes, D. (1988). Representation and processing in the self-system: An action-oriented approach to self and self-relevant phenomena. *Communication Monographs, 55*(4), 287-314.

Gumperz, J., & Hymes, D. (Eds.) (1986). *Directions in sociolinguistics: The ethnography of communication.* New York: Basil Blackwell.

Halfond, M. (1985, November). *Intrapersonal communication—A point of view.* Paper presented at a meeting of the Speech Communication Association, Denver, CO.

Halliday, M. (1970). Language structure and language function. In J. Lyons (Ed.), *New horizons in linguistics* (pp. 140-165). Middlesex, England: Penguin Books.

Harris, R., & Brewer, W. (1973). Deixis in memory for verb tense. *Journal of Verbal Learning and Verbal Behavior, 12*(2), 190-197.

Hartley, E. (Producer). (1974). *Biofeedback: Yoga of the West* [Video]. Cos Cob, CT: Hartley Film Foundation.

Huang, M., & Byrne, B. (1978). Cognitive style and lateral eye movements. *British Journal of Psychology, 69*(1), 85-90.

James, W. (1890). *The principles of psychology I.* New York: Dover Publications.

Joshi, A., Webber, B., & Sag, I. (Eds.). (1981). *Elements of discourse understanding.* Cambridge: Cambridge University Press.

Kinsbourne, M. (1972). Eye and head turning indicates cerebral lateralization. *Science, 176*(4034), 539-541.

Kinsbourne, M. (1974). Direction of gaze and distribution of cerebral thought processes. *Neuropsychologia, 12*(2), 279-281.

Korba, R. (1987). *The rate of inner speech.* Unpublished doctoral dissertation, University of Denver, Denver, CO. *University Microfilms International*, 1987, No. 8629036.

LaFleur, G. (1985, November). *Intrapersonal communication: Problems of contexts and meanings.* Paper presented at a meeting of the Speech Communication Association, Denver, CO.

Labov, W. & Fanshel, D. (1977). *Therapeutic discourse.* New York: Academic Press.

Lakoff, G. & Johnson, M. (1980). *Metaphors we live by.* Chicago: University of Chicago Press.

Langer, S. (1942). *Philosophy in a new key.* New York: New American Library.

Levinson, S. (1983). *Pragmatics.* Cambridge: Cambridge University Press.

Levy, J. (1976). A review of evidence for a genetic component in the determination of handedness. *Behavior Genetics, 6*(4), 429-453.

Littlejohn, S. (1983). *Theories of human communication* (2nd ed.) Belmont, CA: Wadsworth Publishing.

McLaughlin, M. (1984). *How talk is organized.* Beverly Hills, CA: Sage.

Messaris, S., & Gross, L. (1977). Interpretations of a photographic narrative by viewers in four age groups. *Studies in the Anthropology of Visual Communication, 4*(2), 99-111.

Miller, G. (1983). Taking stock of a discipline. *Journal of Communication, 33*(3), 31-41.

Popper, K. (1972). *Objective knowledge: An evolutionary approach.* Oxford: Clarendon Press.

Posner, M. (1973). *Cognition: An introduction.* Glenview, IL: Scott, Foresman.

Raskin V. (1983). *A concise history of linguistic semantics I* (3rd ed.). Unpublished manuscript, Purdue University, West Lafayette, IN.

Reardon, K. (1987). *Where minds meet.* Belmont, CA: Wadsworth.

Richardson, A. (1977). Verbalizer-visualizer: A cognitive style dimension. *Journal of Mental Imagery, 1*(1), 109-126.

Roberts, C. (1983, November). *The definition and delimitation of intrapersonal communication: A physiological perspective.* Paper presented at a meeting of the Speech Communication Association, Washington, DC. [ERIC database: ED 240 634]

Roberts, C., Edwards, R., & Barker, L. (1987). *Intrapersonal communication processes.* Scottsdale, AZ: Gorsuch Scarisbrick.

Roloff, M., & Berger, C. (1982). *Social cognition and communication.* Beverly Hills, CA: Sage.

Ruesch, J., & Bateson, G. (1968). *Communication: The social matrix of psychiatry.* New York: W. W. Norton.

Schulman, A. (1971). Recognition memory for targets from a scanned word list. *British Journal of Psychology, 62*(3), 335-346.

Schweller, K., Brewer, W., & Dahl, D. (1976). Memory for illocutionary forces and perlocutionary effects of utterances. *Journal of Verbal Learning and Verbal Behavior, 15(4),* 325-337.

Scott, M., & Lyman, S. (1968). Accounts. *American Sociological Review, 33*(1), 46-62.

Searle, J. (1969). *Speech acts: An essay in the philosophy of language.* London: Cambridge University Press.

Shedletsky, L. (1989). What evidence do we have for the psychological reality of nonconscious processing? In C. Roberts & K. Watson (Eds.), *Intrapersonal communication processes: Original essays* (pp. 354-379). New Orleans, LA: Spectra.

Slobin, D. (1979). *Psycholinguistics* (2nd ed.). Glenview, IL: Scott, Foresman.

Steil, L., Barker, L., & Watson, K. (1983). *Effective listening.* Reading, MA: Addison-Wesley.

Strause, G., & Ambrester, M. (1986). *Games: Games, activities, measures, exercises in speech.* Salem, WI: Sheffield.

Stubbs, M. (1983). *Discourse analysis: The sociolinguistic analysis of talk.* Oxford: Basil Blackwell.

Tannen, D. (1988). *Conversational style: Analyzing talk among friends.* Norwood, NJ: Ablex.

Vinson, L. (1985, November). *A perspective of intrapersonal communication*. Paper presented at a meeting of the Speech Communication Association, Denver, CO.

Wardhaugh, R. (1986). *How conversation works*. Oxford: Basil Blackwell.

Watzlawick, P., Beavin, J., & Jackson, D. (1967). *Pragmatics of human communication*. New York: W. W. Norton.

Weaver, R., II, & Cotrell, H. (1985, November). *Imaging as intrapersonal communication: A conceptualization*. Paper presented at a meeting of the Speech Communication Association, Denver, CO.

Worth, S., & Gross, L. (1974). Symbolic strategies. *Journal of Communication, 24*(4), 27-39.

Author Index

A

Albee, E.	6
Ambrester, M.	69
Austin, J.	100

B

Bakan, D.	87
Bakan, P.	82
Barker, L.	4, 29, 69, 91
	92, 94, 107
Bateson, G.	92
Beavin, J.	61
Bensen, H.	14
Berger, C.	61, 88, 92
Biddle, P.	91
Billig, M.	97
Block, J.	84, 87
Bock, K.	44
Bode, R.	91
Bookin, H.	105
Bradac, J.	61
Brewer, W.	44, 51, 105
Brown, G.	11
Byrne, B.	83

C

Clark, E.	27
Clark, H.	27, 105
Cofer, C.	65
Coltheart, M.	73
Condon, J.	5, 27, 61
Condor, S.	98
Conrad, R.	71
Cotrell, H.	91
Craig, R.	11
Craik, F.	31, 32
Crawford, L.	16
Cronkhite, G.	101

Crowder, R.	22, 31, 71
Cunningham, S.	92, 93

D

Dahl, D.	105
Dauw, D.	4

E

Edwards, D.	97
Edwards, R.	4, 29, 69, 91, 94

F

Fanshel, D.	11, 104
Fisher, B.	91, 97, 98
Fromkin, V.	25, 27

G

Gane, M.	97
Geddes, D.	70
Gildea, P.	105
Glucksberg, S.	105
Goffman, E.	94
Goss, B.	69, 94
Greene, J.	70
Gross, L.	102
Gumperz, J.	90

H

Halfond, M.	94
Halliday, M.	61
Harris, R.	44, 51
Hartley, E.	30
Honeycutt, J.	4
Huang, M.	83
Hull, E.	73
Hymes, D.	90

J

Jackson, D.	61
James, W.	1
Johnson, M.	98, 99
Joshi, A.	11

K

Kibler, R.	92
Kinsbourne, M.	83
Korba, R.	91

L

Labov, W.	11, 104
LaFleur, G.	92
Lakoff, G.	98, 99
Langer, S.	14
Levinson, S.	11, 102
Levy, J.	82
Lichtenstein, E.	44
Littlejohn, S.	91
Lockhart, R.	31, 32
Lucy, P.	105
Lyman, S.	89

M

McLaughlin, M.	11
Messaris, S.	102
Middleton, D.	97
Miller, G.	96

P

Popper, K.	1
Posner, M.	22, 106

R

Radley, A.	97
Raskin, V.	102
Reardon, K.	91
Richardson, A.	76, 82, 83

Roberts, C.	69, 94
Rodman, R.	25, 27
Roloff, M.	88, 92
Ruesch, J.	92

S

Sag, I.	11
Schulman, A.	32
Schweller, K.	105
Scott, M.	89
Searle, J.	100
Shedletsky, L.	44, 106
Slater, D.	73
Slobin, D.	27
Steil, L.	107
Strause, G.	69
Stubbs, M.	104

T

Tannen, D.	10
Tracy, K.	11

V

Vinson, L.	91

W

Wardhaugh, R.	21
Watson, K.	107
Watzlawick, P.	61
Weaver, R.	91
Webber, B.	11
Worth, S.	102

Y

Yule, G.	11

Z

Zagacki, K.	4

Subject Index

A
Anthropology 95

B
Biofeedback 29, 30

C
Coding Analysis 22, 71-75
Cognition 1, 17, 22, 96
Cognitive Behavior 32
Cognitive Psychology 95
Cognitive Style 76-78, 82, 83
Concept Formation 61-68, 102
Concept Identification 61-68
Conversational Analysis 14

D
Deixis 51, 52
Discourse Analysis 14, 95

E
Exteroception 92
Exterotransmission 92

H
Heightened Sensation 14

I
Information Processing 32
Interpersonal
 Communication 10, 16
Involuntary Naming 14

L
Linguistic Communication 107
Linguistics 27, 95

M
Metacognition 1

P
Philosophy 95
Pragmatics 10, 44, 95, 103
Proprioception 92
Propriotransmission 92
Psychological Time 14

R
Relaxation 14, 30

S
Semantics 31, 103
Speech 95
Speech Communication 95
Stage Analysis 22, 31
Subconscious 23

T
Task Analysis 22

V
Verbal Coding 71-75
Verbal Processing 82
Visual Coding 71-75
Visual Processing 82